GETTING ALONG WITH PEOPLE

DIANNE DOUBTFIRE is a professional novelist. She has written novels for adults and teenagers, and two guides for writers. She also enjoys teaching creative writing. Her first book in the Overcoming Common Problems series, *Overcoming Shyness – A Woman's Guide*, was published by Sheldon in 1989. She lives with her husband in Hampshire.

Overcoming Common Problems Series

For a full list of titles please contact
Sheldon Press, Marylebone Road, London NW1 4DU

Beating Job Burnout
DR DONALD SCOTT

Beating the Blues
SUSAN TANNER AND JILLIAN
BALL

Being the Boss
STEPHEN FITZSIMON

Birth Over Thirty
SHEILA KITZINGER

Body Language
How to read others' thoughts by their
gestures
ALLAN PEASE

Bodypower
DR VERNON COLEMAN

Bodysense
DR VERNON COLEMAN

Calm Down
How to cope with frustration and anger
DR PAUL HAUCK

Changing Course
How to take charge of your career
SUE DYSON AND STEPHEN HOARE

Comfort for Depression
JANET HORWOOD

Complete Public Speaker
GYLES BRANDRETH

**Coping Successfully with Your Child's
Asthma**
DR PAUL CARSON

**Coping Successfully with Your Hyperactive
Child**
DR PAUL CARSON

**Coping Successfully with Your Irritable
Bowel**
ROSEMARY NICOL

Coping with Anxiety and Depression
SHIRLEY TRICKETT

Coping with Blushing
DR ROBERT EDELMANN

Coping with Cot Death
SARAH MURPHY

Coping with Depression and Elation
DR PATRICK McKEON

Coping with Stress
DR GEORGIA WITKIN-LANOIL

Coping with Suicide
DR DONALD SCOTT

Coping with Thrush
CAROLINE CLAYTON

Curing Arthritis – The Drug-Free Way
MARGARET HILLS

Curing Arthritis Diet Book
MARGARET HILLS

**Curing Coughs, Colds and Flu – The
Drug-Free Way**
MARGARET HILLS

Curing Illness – The Drug-Free Way
MARGARET HILLS

Depression
DR PAUL HAUCK

Divorce and Separation
ANGELA WILLANS

Don't Blame Me!
How to stop blaming yourself
and other people
TONY GOUGH

The Epilepsy Handbook
SHELAGH McGOVERN

**Everything You Need to Know about
Adoption**
MAGGIE JONES

**Everything You Need to Know about
Contact Lenses**
DR ROBERT YOUNGSON

**Everything You Need to Know about
Osteoporosis**
ROSEMARY NICOL

Overcoming Common Problems Series

Everything You Need to Know about Shingles
DR ROBERT YOUNGSON

Everything You Need to Know about Your Eyes
DR ROBERT YOUNGSON

Family First Aid and Emergency Handbook
DR ANDREW STANWAY

Feverfew
A traditional herbal remedy for migraine and arthritis
DR STEWART JOHNSON

Fight Your Phobia and Win
DAVID LEWIS

Getting Along with People
DIANNE DOUBTFIRE

Getting Married
JOANNA MOORHEAD

Goodbye Backache
DR DAVID IMRIE WITH COLLEEN DIMSON

Heart Attacks – Prevent and Survive
DR TOM SMITH

Helping Children Cope with Divorce
ROSEMARY WELLS

Helping Children Cope with Grief
ROSEMARY WELLS

Helping Children Cope with Stress
URSULA MARKHAM

Hold Your Head Up High
DR PAUL HAUCK

How to be a Successful Secretary
SUE DYSON AND STEPHEN HOARE

How to Be Your Own Best Friend
DR PAUL HAUCK

How to Control your Drinking
DRS W. MILLER AND R. MUNOZ

How to Cope with Stress
DR PETER TYRER

How to Cope with Tinnitus and Hearing Loss
DR ROBERT YOUNGSON

How to Cope with Your Child's Allergies
DR PAUL CARSON

How to Cure Your Ulcer
ANNE CHARLISH AND DR BRIAN GAZZARD

How to Do What You Want to Do
DR PAUL HAUCK

How to Get Things Done
ALISON HARDINGHAM

How to Improve Your Confidence
DR KENNETH HAMBLY

How to Interview and Be Interviewed
MICHELE BROWN AND GYLES BRANDRETH

How to Love a Difficult Man
NANCY GOOD

How to Love and be Loved
DR PAUL HAUCK

How to Make Successful Decisions
ALISON HARDINGHAM

How to Move House Successfully
ANNE CHARLISH

How to Pass Your Driving Test
DONALD RIDLAND

How to Say No to Alcohol
KEITH McNEILL

How to Spot Your Child's Potential
CECILE DROUIN AND ALAIN DUBOS

How to Stand up for Yourself
DR PAUL HAUCK

How to Start a Conversation and Make Friends
DON GABOR

How to Stop Smoking
GEORGE TARGET

How to Stop Taking Tranquillisers
DR PETER TYRER

How to Stop Worrying
DR FRANK TALLIS

How to Study Successfully
MICHELE BROWN

Overcoming Common Problems Series

Hysterectomy
SUZIE HAYMAN

Jealousy
DR PAUL HAUCK

Learning from Experience
A woman's guide to getting
older without panic
PATRICIA O'BRIEN

Learning to Live with Multiple Sclerosis
DR ROBERT POVEY, ROBIN DOWIE
AND GILLIAN PRETT

Living Alone – A Woman's Guide
LIZ McNEILL TAYLOR

Living Through Personal Crisis
ANN KAISER STEARNS

Living with Grief
DR TONY LAKE

Living with High Blood Pressure
DR TOM SMITH

Loneliness
DR TONY LAKE

Making Marriage Work
DR PAUL HAUCK

Making the Most of Loving
GILL COX AND SHEILA DAINOW

Making the Most of Yourself
GILL COX AND SHEILA DAINOW

Managing Two Careers
How to survive as a working mother
PATRICIA O'BRIEN

Meeting People is Fun
How to overcome shyness
DR PHYLLIS SHAW

Menopause
RAEWYN MACKENZIE

The Nervous Person's Companion
DR KENNETH HAMBLY

Overcoming Fears and Phobias
DR TONY WHITEHEAD

Overcoming Shyness
A woman's guide
DIANNE DOUBTFIRE

Overcoming Stress
DR VERNON COLEMAN

Overcoming Tension
DR KENNETH HAMBLY

Overcoming Your Nerves
DR TONY LAKE

The Parkinson's Disease Handbook
DR RICHARD GODWIN-AUSTEN

Say When!
Everything a woman needs to know about
alcohol and drinking problems
ROSEMARY KENT

Self-Help for your Arthritis
EDNA PEMBLE

Slay Your Own Dragons
How women can overcome
self-sabotage in love and work
NANCY GOOD

Sleep Like a Dream – The Drug-Free Way
ROSEMARY NICOL

Solving your Personal Problems
PETER HONEY

A Special Child in the Family
Living with your sick or disabled child
DIANA KIMPTON

Think Your Way to Happiness
DR WINDY DRYDEN AND JACK GORDO

Trying to Have a Baby?
Overcoming infertility and child loss
MAGGIE JONES

Why Be Afraid?
How to overcome your fears
DR PAUL HAUCK

Women and Depression
A practical self-help guide
DEIDRE SANDERS

You and Your Varicose Veins
DR PATRICIA GILBERT

Your Arthritic Hip and You
GEORGE TARGET

Your Grandchild and You
ROSEMARY WELLS

Overcoming Common Problems

GETTING ALONG
WITH PEOPLE

Dianne Doubtfire

SHELDON PRESS
LONDON

First published in Great Britain in 1990 by
Sheldon Press, SPCK, Marylebone Road, London NW1 4DU

Second impression 1992

British Library Cataloguing in Publication Data
Doubtfire, Dianne
    Getting along with people. – (Overcoming common
    problems)
    1. Interpersonal relationships. Communication –
    Manuals
    I. Title   II. Series
    302.2

    ISBN 0–85969–600–6

Typeset by Deltatype Ltd, Ellesmere Port, Cheshire
Printed and Bound in Great Britain by
Courier International Limited, East Kilbride

For Sheila Bishop
a friend for all seasons

To profit from good advice requires more
wisdom than to give it.
JOHN CHURTON COLLINS

Also by Dianne Doubtfire

Novels
Lust for Innocence
Reason for Violence
Kick a Tin Can
The Flesh is Strong
Behind the Screen
The Wrong Face

Novels for Teenagers
Escape on Monday
This Jim
Girl in Cotton Wool
A Girl Called Rosemary
Sky Girl
Girl in a Gondola
Sky Lovers

Non-Fiction
The Craft of Novel-Writing
Teach Yourself Creative Writing
Overcoming Shyness: A Woman's Guide

Contents

Acknowledgements

The author and publishers are grateful to the following authors and publishers for permission to quote copyright material:

BBC Television for an extract from Bertrand Russell's *Face to Face* interview with John Freeman.

William Heinemann Ltd for an extract from *Staying On* by Paul Scott.

Macdonald Optima for an extract from *All in the Mind?* by Dr Brian Roet.

Prentice-Hall Inc for excerpts from *Psycho-Cybernetics* by Maxwell Maltz, MD, FICS.

Souvenir Press Ltd for excerpts from *The Silva Mind Control Method* by José Silva and Philip Miele.

Unwin Hyman Ltd for an extract from *Self Mastery through Conscious Autosuggestion* by Emile Coué.

The author and publishers also acknowledge the use of quotations from *The Guardian* and *Yours*.

The author would like to extend warm personal thanks to the following for their generous help and advice: Sheila Bishop, Dorothy Branco, Stanley Doubtfire, Ann Dymond, Rosalind Jones, Ann Kennington, Tessa Krailing and the Isle of Wight New Writers' Group, Ena Richards, Dick Richards, Sita Sheer, Barbara Tims, Valerie Wilding and the Haslemere Writers' Group.

Introduction

One of the greatest human needs is to communicate with our fellows, to understand and to be understood. In earliest infancy we scream the message to our mothers that we are thirsty, frightened or in pain. If we are not understood or if our demands go unheeded, we are miserable. To be attended to and have our needs satisfied, is bliss. And this, to a large extent, is the story of our lives. We want things, need things, fear things, and if we have no-one to understand us we are not only frustrated and unhappy but we may grow sick as well.

Getting along with people – friends, relations, colleagues at work and total strangers – means a great many things, but most of all, perhaps, it means trying to understand them and sympathize with their problems. It also means communicating our own feelings in such a way that we do not cause offence or distress. Getting along with those who are happy and well balanced is usually easy; difficult people, interesting and dynamic as they may be, represent a challenge. We must accept the challenge if we are to feel at home in the world. Bad relationships cause nervous tension and undermine our self-esteem, so we must surely make a special effort to get along with people who are not easy to understand.

Happy relationships require goodwill and perseverance, and although there will always be problems if other people are bent on causing friction, there is a great deal we can do if we genuinely seek for harmony and are prepared to make a few concessions. I would never advocate peace at any price – that would undermine our self-respect – but many disagreements can only be resolved by compromise and sometimes we have to give way a little.

We've all been put together on this amazing ball in space, whether we like it or not. If we can establish rapport with people, making new friends, cementing bonds that already exist, bearing no grudges against those who have hurt us, we are bound to find our stay on this planet a great deal more enjoyable.

Perhaps the most important lesson I have learnt in my later years is that many people are very different from me, in background, personality and outlook, and that I must be tolerant of those differences. Everyone has a right to his or her own attitudes and if others are intolerant, that's no reason for me to be. We can't expect to get along with *all* the people *all* the time, but I think we should be able to manage it most of the time and to get much better at it as the years go by. That's what this book is about.

Dianne Doubtfire, 1989

1

Conversation

Conversation, of course, means a great deal more than the mere exchange of words. It embraces smiles and glances, tender touches, whispers and laughter. It may also include sighs and frowns, shouts and screams and angry blows. And silence. Silence can be one of the most significant forms of communication, both loving and antagonistic.

But this book is about getting along with people and, although from time to time we must all express dissent and even justifiable rage, my theme is the search for understanding in our personal relationships. This can best be achieved, I think, by honesty tempered with humour and compassion. Perhaps the most important requirement is to try to identify with the other person, to look at his or her problems with sympathy. (To avoid the continual use of 'his or her' and 'he and she', I'll settle for 'her' and 'she' to imply either sex.) If we can manage to picture ourselves in another person's place – and it's far from easy, of course – our words will rarely be punctuated with scowls and condemnation. I say 'rarely' because I don't want to give the impression that we shouldn't stand up strongly against injustice. 'For evil to triumph,' said Edmund Burke, 'it is only necessary for good men to do nothing.' There will be occasions when, in order to get along with people of good will, we must speak out fearlessly against the troublemakers.

We shall sometimes encounter people we do not even *wish* to get along with, destructive and hurtful people who, for some reason, will not respond to kindliness however patiently we try to understand them. We must always bear in mind that a hard and intransigent person may be suffering from some deep-seated neurosis that could be eased beyond measure by a genuinely sympathetic approach. We all know how upset we can feel when someone speaks to us in a cold, harsh or indifferent tone of voice, and how pleasant and reassuring it is to be addressed with warmth and interest, whether by an old friend or a stranger. The vast majority of people respond to kindliness as we do ourselves, but if we are obliged to live or work with a difficult person who will not or cannot be pleasant, it is in our own interest as well as theirs to make a sustained effort to find common ground and avoid friction as far as possible. In chapter 7 ('Difficult Relationships') we shall consider this problem in detail.

Choice of words

In all our conversations we must try to ensure that we convey the meaning we intend. Misunderstandings can often be avoided if we take care to choose the right words. When we talk to a small child we naturally use a simple vocabulary that she can understand. In conversing with adults we are sometimes thoughtless in this respect. We all know the irritation we feel when confronted with complex legal documents which seem to be specially designed to confuse us, and yet we could ourselves be guilty of using technical terms to people who are not familiar with our particular jargon. When I'm teaching Creative Writing in Adult Education classes I have to be careful to explain such expressions as present participle and the pluperfect tense because many of my students haven't thought much about grammar since their schooldays. A friend of mine recently told a joke at a party about what happened to his distributor cap and half the group were bored to tears because they didn't know what he was talking about. Sailing enthusiasts tell stories about sheets and stays and painters and burgees that mean nothing to a landlubber. If you're a computer buff or a civil servant, for instance, you'll need to be careful not to confuse those of us who are outside your field.

Another problem is bad language. Most of us swear a little from time to time as a matter of course, but we have to be careful not to offend anyone who may be a little old-fashioned or over-sensitive in this respect. My own vocabulary is far from pure; I learnt a number of swear words in the Air Force that seem to have stuck, but I do try to avoid them unless I'm with friends who know me and don't object.

We often say that So-and-So 'doesn't speak the same language'. When someone differs radically in their religious or political views from us it isn't easy to communicate happily on those levels because our emotions are closely involved. That's why it's unwise to argue about such matters at a party. Having broken this rule myself with disastrous results I recommend you to be aware of the dangers, especially if the wine is flowing freely. Alcohol can make us too outspoken or too quick to take offence.

Body language

The very way you sit conveys a message. If you turn partly away from the person you are talking to, fiddle with your fingers, tap your foot or in any way move restlessly, you are bound to give the impression that you are not really interested in the conversation. Relaxation is the secret, both mental and physical; if we relax our minds, devoting ourselves entirely to the matter in hand, we shall encourage our bodies to relax as well. Conversely, relaxed muscles produce a calm attitude of mind. Jumpy movements and nervous mannerisms are a barrier to satisfactory conversation because they distract attention from the words being spoken. The practice of deep relaxation for two fifteen-minute periods every day can work a near-miracle (see chapter 9).

Do try not to yawn when someone is talking to you. It can be a symptom of nervous tension as well as boredom or fatigue, and it's bound to spoil the atmosphere. If you are so tired that you can't control it, explain and apologise.

Eye contact

This is perhaps the most important aspect of body language. It's almost impossible to get along with someone if you don't look at them. If someone is avoiding my eye, gazing around, looking over my shoulder or down at their hands, I get the feeling that they are bored or impatient and I lose concentration. I'm sure you feel the same. It's often shyness that makes people resist eye contact, but with patience we can improve. We *must* look people in the eye when we are talking to them to show our interest and friendliness. Needless to say, we must also avoid staring fixedly and continuously; that would be embarrassing. But if you have a kind of inborn reticence which prevents you from looking into a person's eyes from time to time, I think you should be able to train yourself to overcome this. At first you'll have to make a deliberate effort, but gradually it will become more natural and you'll be rewarded with a feeling of greater ease and comfort.

Those who lack self-esteem often feel that they don't want to reveal themselves, that people who look into their eyes will see their soul, but the more we try to hide our true selves away the more unhappy we become. Openness and honesty are endearing qualities. Normal eye contact establishes your good faith, whereas a shifty glance gives the impression that you have something to hide.

Talking to strangers

Fear of the unknown is a factor in all our lives, and strangers may inhibit us for no reason other than not knowing what to expect of them. We have to remember that they probably feel the same about us and we must make every effort to remove their apprehensions and put them at their ease. This is the surest way of feeling at ease ourselves.

A friendly smile, I think, is the first essential. We all know how much more relaxed we feel when we are greeted cheerfully. A cool, unwelcoming stare, from a shop assistant for instance, even though it may be unintentional, can make me turn on my heel and shop elsewhere. But that's intolerance on my part. It isn't easy to smile if you are feeling unwell or depressed. Good relationships with strangers require an effort on both sides; if we can be the ones to set the standard, as it were, we shall nearly always be rewarded.

Conversational gambits can seem difficult for those who are inclined to be shy, and this means that two shy people might never get to know one another. Just as it takes two to make a quarrel, it also takes two to engage in a rewarding dialogue. Why not resolve to master the art of opening a conversation? You'll find it well worth while, and it isn't so difficult once you've overcome your initial reserve.

Parties present a problem to many people, but if we find ourselves sitting or standing next to someone who is obviously feeling uneasy, it's up to us, for their sakes as well as our own, to start the ball rolling. A good opening is: 'I'm afraid I get a bit nervy on these occasions. Do you?' If the other person feels the same you have established a fellow feeling, and a good relationship is likely to follow. If your neighbour *doesn't* get nervy (or says she doesn't) then she is honour bound to prove it and will begin to talk!

I think it's best to avoid arguments when we are talking to strangers. Some people are very easily hurt and it isn't until you know someone quite well that you can gauge the likely response to a controversial comment. There are those who revel in the cut and thrust of an argument, and those who find it painful and embarrassing.

Whatever you do, don't moan! I was at a party recently and found myself pinned in a corner with a man who talked about nothing but the trouble he'd had to park his car, his 'flu virus which was still hanging on after three months, his problems with the plumber, and the awful weather. I encouraged him to tell me about his work, but that was a tale of woe as well. At last I got him on to his favourite television programmes and it wasn't long before we were laughing together at some recollections of *Fawlty Towers*. Nevertheless, I didn't stay with him for any longer than necessary. We must always avoid attitudes and comments that mark us down as dreary unfortunates. Cheerfulness and optimism are winners in the human relationship stakes; complaints and pessimism are sure losers.

When we meet people who are bent on negative talk we must obviously be sympathetic, but try to steer the conversation along more pleasing lines.

When you have begun a conversation there is no better way of moving forward successfully than to ask about interests and hobbies, being prepared to open your mind to new subjects and strange ideas. Everyone has a main interest: cooking, gardening, sport, animals, cars, theatre, books, films, music, astronomy, local government, interior decoration, family matters, finance, the environment, to name but a few. . . . It's very likely that one of your own specialities is in that list. As I have suggested earlier, religion and politics, although they are of deep interest to many people, are too controversial to be a wise choice for an opening gambit.

I would advise against asking people, in the early stages of a conversation, if they are married or if they have any children. There may be a sad story of illness, divorce or bereavement attached to the answer. On the other hand, if someone asks *you* a painful question, try to answer cheerfully and explain without embarrassment, making the questioner feel that you don't mind talking freely and honestly about the problem. Deep friendships often grow from such beginnings. Once you have got into conversation with a stranger you may find you can talk very freely indeed; in fact it's often easier to discuss emotional issues with someone who doesn't know you very well.

I wrote the following article for *The Guardian* newspaper in 1988 and had many appreciative letters from people in similar situations.

It used to be a question I loved to hear: 'Have you any children?'

'Yes,' I would reply, 'I've a son; he's a chorister at Chichester Cathedral.' Or later: 'Yes, my son's a hanggliding instructor; he runs his own school. He's just flown off the top of Kilimanjaro.' The latest happy answer was: 'Yes, he's just got married', and I would bring out the photographs.

Then, in 1983, he died after a short illness. He was 34. But of course some stranger will inevitably ask the familiar question – a new hairdresser, someone in the supermarket, a student in one of my classes. I have to tell them. And there will never be an end to it.

So what am I trying to say? That people shouldn't ask that question in case the reply is not a happy one? No, of course I'm not. It's a lovely question, one I have often asked and shall go on asking, because it usually brings forth a proud response.

A mother of happy children likes nothing better than to talk about them and to produce photographs. But now I realise, as I never did before, that there are many mothers who cannot, for any one of a hundred reasons, answer with pleasure.

But what is the solution? I think we have to try to answer it with equanimity and without embarrassment, probably finding, as I have often done, a new and caring friend. It is only when we suffer misfortunes of our own that we really understand the meaning of compassion. It takes a person with problems fully to comprehend another's and, since our son died, I have attained a maturity I did not know I lacked. People's bereavements used to make me nervous but not any more; now I know what to say and how to say it.

There is obviously no escape from this friendly, innocent question; it will always have to be faced. If we can learn to answer it calmly and positively, we shall fear it less, suffer less, embarrass others less and possibly gain the opportunity to offer comfort in return. When people hear of our sorrows, they feel they can speak more freely of their own.

'I've never been able to talk to anyone like this before,' a woman told me in the post office queue, 'I feel better already.' She had recently lost her daughter in a road accident. I think it's important to help the questioner not to feel guilty at having asked the question. I always say: 'Don't worry – I like to talk about him.' This is true; it's so much healthier to speak openly than to treat the loss as a taboo subject.

In many ways I am lucky because our son had a happy and adventurous life and spent his last year married to the girl he loved. He has left us a wealth of marvellous memories and these are the blessings I talk of when I am asked that difficult question.

Travelling

Some people, myself included, think of a journey as a great opportunity to catch up on some reading; a talkative stranger can sometimes be an intrusion on one's privacy. Just to sit in a train and look out of the window can be bliss for, say, a teacher or for someone who lives with an incessant talker. Let's consider both sides of the travel situation. If you're the one who wants to read, I think it's best to say so, after a few pleasantries, and turn to your book. If, on the other hand, you want to talk and you receive a less than enthusiastic response, don't be offended. Some people are inclined to take it personally if their neighbour on a bus, train or plane prefers to read, look out of the window or snooze rather than talk. All we need, I think, is to be sensitive to people's individual wishes and do our best not to intrude.

A final word about the hazards of talking to strangers. Women must obviously be very careful indeed, but getting along with potential muggers and rapists is outside the scope of this book!

I can tell you, however, of a personal experience which might be a useful guide for a woman in a threatening situation. I had been to the theatre and was travelling alone on the London Underground. It was nearly 11 p.m. and I felt uneasy when my woman friend got out at her station and I found myself alone in the carriage. At the next stop four unsavoury-looking men got in, slouched across to where I was sitting and virtually surrounded me, eyeing me with open menace and edging closer. I was, of course, absolutely terrified, but I managed to face them (I hoped) with a friendly and fearless gaze and said conversationally, 'You're just the

10

guys I need to give me a bit of expert information. Do you understand the offside rule in Soccer?'

They were obviously thrown, and we should never forget that surprise is a valuable weapon on such occasions. The most evil-looking of the four men, dirty and fat, grunted and nodded to one of his mates. So I went on, 'Could you explain it to me, please? I love watching football but I've never understood that rule.' (This, in fact, is true – and to this day I don't really understand it!) One man began to tell me, the fat one joined in and – can you believe it? – those four men were soon arguing amongst themselves about the offside rule and how to put it across to me. The train drew in to my station while they were still disagreeing, so I thanked them and got out, shaking at the knees and overcoming an impulse to run like mad for the exit. Luckily, such situations seldom arise, and possibly the men wanted nothing but the amusement of scaring me. I shall never know.

Strangers, most of the time, are simply other human beings who, like ourselves, want only to be liked and understood.

2

Listening

Listening – *really* listening – is a very special skill. It may not be a natural skill but it's one that can be developed. Children under school age aren't usually very good at it, unless they're having a story read to them or hearing about a present or a treat in store. Subconsciously, however, they listen to adult conversation or they would never pick up their native language so quickly. In the classroom they *have* to listen, from time to time, to lessons that hold very little interest for them, and this is excellent training for later life when we must concentrate on monologues we could very well do without.

Small children, as a rule, are chiefly interested in themselves; most of us grow out of this as the years go by – though not entirely! We can listen with pleasure to words of praise, to entertaining friends, a good radio programme or advice on making money, but we are inclined to lose concentration when people tell us dreary anecdotes about themselves or about someone we have never heard of. ('Was it Tuesday or Wednesday? Let me think – no, it was Tuesday because I had to collect a prescription for my uncle. It's his leg – it's never been right since . . .', etc.)

A tedious dissertation such as this makes listening very difficult but if we intervene with a question or a comment we can often guide the conversation along more rewarding lines. Good listening demands tolerance and understanding, but we shouldn't be too submissive and allow ourselves to be used as a sounding board by those who are too fond of hearing their own voices. Don't hesitate to arrest the flow ('Just a sec. – it's my turn now!').

There are two kinds of listening, however: active and passive. We must make up our minds, according to the circumstances, whether the conversation is a normal 'give-and-take' or whether we should encourage someone to unburden themselves to us. People who chatter to excess may be concealing some hidden pain or neurosis and it often helps them to talk about it. If we can persuade a timid person to express herself more fully and forcefully we may do her a great service. The airing of hopes and fears can help someone to feel more confident and self-assured, and deepening the friendship improves communication.

People sometimes speak quietly about an issue of great importance to them, and a heartfelt plea for understanding may be ignored unless the listener is truly attentive. A woman I know tried for days to tell her husband that she was worried in case their son was taking drugs. He wouldn't listen – partly, I think, because he was jealous of his wife's concern; the boy was, in fact, experimenting with heroin and very much in need of his parents' help. Another example is the problem of Clare, a girl in her twenties, who tried unsuccessfully to make her mother listen when she wanted to admit she was pregnant. She had a great need for sympathy and advice but her mother's lack of involvement drove her to attempt suicide.

On some occasions, when there is no positive action to be taken, a person who is lonely, grieving or in pain may need nothing so much as a friend who will sit beside her, holding her hand perhaps, nodding sympathetically from time to time but saying little except to offer an occasional comforting word.

Listening is obviously an essential part of conversation. However passionately we may need to express our own ideas and air our problems, we should always break off frequently to hear the other person's views, to ask questions or just to provide a little quietude. Continual talk can produce nervous tension and we need not feel impelled to say *anything*, no matter what, to fill a silence. Silences can be restful and pleasant so long as neither party feels embarrassed by them. If your companion insists on talking all the time, why not smile and say (quite firmly) that you'd like to close your eyes and relax for a few minutes.

There is probably no more important factor in human

relationships than listening to people with kindly attention, however young or old they are, and however much we would really like to go away and get on with our own lives. Everyone loves a good listener and we never know when we ourselves may need the comfort of someone with a patient and sympathetic ear.

Making people feel good

I know it's asking a lot sometimes, but I do think we should try to make people feel better about themselves if we possibly can, avoiding recriminations and carping criticism. Friendliness depends a great deal on self-assurance and if we can bring out the best in others we shall also develop the best in ourselves. We should do our utmost to avoid making anyone feel guilty, unloved or humiliated. This doesn't mean, of course, that we shouldn't feel free to criticize the bad behaviour of friends and relations; it means that we should try to understand the causes of such behaviour and concentrate on seeing the best in people. You may think this is far too idealistic a view for the 1990s but I make no apology for being an idealist. It's impossible to live up to our high ideals all the time, but at least we can keep them constantly in mind. Without them we are lost.

Many of my readers will love, as I do, this prayer of St Francis of Assisi: '. . . grant that I may not so much seek to be consoled as to console; to be understood as to understand; to be loved, as to love; for it is in giving that we receive, it is in pardoning that we are pardoned . . .'. Surely a first-class recipe for getting along with people!

If we genuinely want to understand, rather than be understood, all manner of happy times are in store for us. New friendships will bloom, existing ones will deepen and old enmities magically melt away. You will probably know from experience that this is no airy-fairy speculation, but the truth, based on unchanging principles.

An important aspect of making people feel good is not to

implant negative suggestions. For instance, I feel very strongly that we should never tell anyone they look tired. To say, 'You look tired' is like saying, 'You look awful' and the poor person (especially a woman) will feel even worse than before. It's often said, of course, and with the best of sympathetic intentions, but if you say instead, 'You must be tired' and follow it up with an offer of help – a cup of tea, a drink, a plumped up cushion or a footstool – this can be a great comfort.

Many years ago, when I broke my leg, a friend told me that it would always be painful in wet weather. I worried about it (quite needlessly, as it happens) and I think we should avoid pessimistic talk of that nature. Many doctors are far from blameless in this respect, as you may know. The power of the mind is tremendous, and anxiety, especially if it's engendered by a figure of authority, can bring about the very thing we dread, just as faith and optimism can promote good health in the most unlikely circumstances. Always offer comfort and encouragement whenever possible; good cheer is infectious.

Gossip is death to happy friendships. I think we should take people as *we ourselves* find them, not as other people may have found them. I learnt this years ago when I believed a lie I was told about a friend, and behaved coolly towards her as a result. When I discovered the lie I apologized, of course, but our easy comradeship was lost beyond recall. And what about the woman who told the lie in the first place? As a great believer in the direct approach, I faced her with the situation. She broke down and wept, insisting she had believed the lie to be the truth. She then agreed with me that tales of that nature should never be repeated. In fact I don't believe in passing on unpleasant tales about anyone, true or doubtful, unless it is essential for someone's safety or peace of mind. And I certainly think we should give everyone the benefit of the doubt on all occasions. After all, isn't that what we want for ourselves? Trust is a top priority for good relationships and we should always give it until it is betrayed. Many of my readers will disagree and we must all make our own decisions on these delicate matters, but trust breeds trust, just as suspicion breeds suspicion.

Some people don't seem to *want* to feel good. They have probably been put down so much by parents, teachers, husbands, wives or lovers that they have a poor self-image and can't believe that they deserve affection or praise. We should make a special effort to build up the confidence of anyone who is shy or guilt-ridden. People are inclined to become what they believe themselves to be, and if you go on telling yourself that you are lazy, clumsy, forgetful, nervous or any one of a hundred negative attributes, it's more than likely that you will develop those faults to a greater degree. Instead, if you assert that your health is improving, that you are becoming less nervous, more energetic, etc, you will become so. You probably know that phrase of Emile Coué's: 'Day by day in every way I'm getting better and better'. Sadly, it is often looked on as a bit of a joke, but thousands of people have been cured of serious complaints simply by repeating that phrase twenty times every morning and evening. I do it myself, and I rely to a very large degree on positive thinking to keep me well and happy.

Nobody, however beautiful, brilliant or successful, is ever completely self-assured. We have only to remember the tragic story of Marilyn Monroe to realize that beauty, wealth and fame, far from ensuring happiness, can sometimes undermine it. Everyone feels insecure and helpless on certain occasions, longing for comfort and reassurance. Let us be the ones to give it whenever possible, listening patiently and making those around us feel relaxed and happy. We may feel sometimes that they hardly deserve it, but a harmonious atmosphere is conducive to good communication, and that's what getting along with people is all about.

3

The Telephone

Many people are nervous of the telephone; they see it as some kind of monster there to confound them, rather than a miraculous instrument for making contact with people one might not otherwise have a chance to talk to. Far-away friends are suddenly right beside you, their voices as warm and lively as if they were in the same room. The telephone should be a servant and a helpmate, not a tyrant, and it's mainly up to us what use we make of it. If others use it to torment us – unsolicited advertising, difficult and persistent friends and relatives, not to mention heavy breathers! – we must deal with them calmly but very firmly indeed.

Most of the time, however, phoning can be a pleasure, and never is the tone of our voice more important than when we can't be seen and there are no smiles and gestures to convey our friendliness. They say a smile can be 'heard' on the telephone, and we need to make a special effort to sound sympathetic. 'But I might not be *feeling* sympathetic,' you could argue; 'I might want to show somebody who's boss and blow my top.' All right, but in this book we're applying ourselves to getting along with people, and showing who's boss might not help!

Some people sound unfriendly on the phone when in fact they are nothing of the kind. They have a rather brusque, off-putting manner, possibly to show that they are very busy people with no time to waste. This may be necessary in some cases to discourage the moaners and wafflers who have nothing much to say, but if you feel you have a tendency to sound intimidating, why not make a determined effort to adopt a mellower approach?

My own problem is that I speak too loudly, especially when I'm excited. I continually remind myself to lower my voice, and apparently I'm improving, so if this is a failing of yours, it's worth making the effort. I also have a tendency to interrupt, and I'm working on that as well. We really should allow people to finish a sentence before we break in, although in some cases we'd hardly get a word in edgeways if we did.

Let's consider answering the phone. Some people give their numbers, others say 'Hello', some grunt; I prefer to announce myself at once so that the caller knows who he or she is talking to. 'Dianne Doubtfire' I say in a friendly tone (yes, even in the middle of a snooker final, though I must admit it takes some doing!). You've got to remember that you, too, sometimes ring people at a difficult time, but you don't expect a dusty answer, do you? The same applies to wrong numbers. We really shouldn't be bad-tempered when someone says: 'Is that the Chinese take-away?' or: 'Can I speak to Porky?'. Of course it's irritating, especially if it was a problem getting to the phone, but haven't *we* ever got anybody out of the bath by mistake? Wrong numbers are usually the result of carelessness but not always; Telecom computers aren't infallible. So let's be pleasant about it if we get a false alarm and also let's apologize warmly if we are the guilty party.

I'll tell you a lovely story, absolutely true, about a wrong number. A friend of mine discovered one morning that her cat was sick. She phoned the vet and went into a long description of the cat's (rather unsavoury) symptoms. She then asked if she should bring the cat to the surgery. This was the reply: 'Well, I'm afraid you've got the wrong number. This is Robson's Electronics Limited.' My friend, who has a great sense of humour, came back with: 'Oh, so you can't help me about my cat, then?' 'Not unless she's got something wrong with her electrics', was the reply. Now *that's* the kind of wrong number that gets the day off to a good start!

I sometimes have a problem when an acquaintance phones me and says: 'Hello – this is Ann' or: 'Hi, this is Mike'. I know quite a number of Anns and Mikes, and as my ear for voices isn't very good I might have to say 'Ann who?' or 'Which Mike?' This must be a bit off-putting for the poor caller, so I think it's best to give your surname as well unless the person you're phoning is certain to know who you are – or unless you have an unusual name like Peregrine or Amaryllis!

When you phone someone and want to talk for several minutes, it's a good idea to ask if it's convenient or would they rather that you called back later. If they say, 'Yes please' then arrange a time and make a note of it. Do keep a pad and pencil by the telephone; it's maddening for both of you if you have to rush away to find one. If someone phones you at a difficult moment, don't hesitate to explain and say you'll ring back later. Fix a time and be sure you don't forget. I rely on my kitchen pinger a great deal, not only when I'm cooking.

At the start of a call I think the classic 'How are you?' is a good opening. After all, you don't want to invite someone to a party if they've just broken a leg or lost a close relative. I know it's dangerous to ask some people how they are because they'll tell you for half an hour if you let them, but I think it has to be done. Listen sympathetically, of course, if the news is bad, making positive comments wherever possible and changing the subject gently if they go on too long.

Try to keep your own complaints to a minimum. If you really need comfort, the telephone is a wonderful blessing, but we should avoid going on about our problems unless it's really necessary. I knew a woman who always talked at such length about her ailments that I avoided ringing her and dreaded her phoning me. Moaners never get along with people very well, either on the phone or off it.

Don't prolong a call any more than you need to, regardless of who is paying for it. I know someone who rambles on at such length that I can lay the receiver down, go off and pour myself a drink and when I come back she'll still be talking, not knowing that I've been away!

Don't ring anybody after 9.30 p.m. unless it's really necessary. For you it may seem early but people who get up at the crack of dawn (and I'm one of them) often need an early night. Likewise, don't risk waking anyone up before 7.45 a.m. – that still gives you time to take advantage of the cheap rate. If you know a person's sleeping routine, do respect it. I have a friend who never surfaces before 11 a.m. and another who writes his novels all through the night, going to bed at 6 a.m. and getting up at 2 p.m. If you phone a foreign country take account of the time difference, or you might ring someone in the middle of the night.

I would suggest that you never hang up in a temper. You are, on some occasions, quite justifiably going to feel angry, but it's best to keep calm and avoid upsetting your nervous system. If you don't, you will cause problems for yourself as well as the caller. For one thing, you will anticipate a come-back, and every time the phone rings you'll be liable to get that sick feeling in the pit of your stomach. And you'll probably dislike yourself for losing control and regret your hastiness. Most important of all, you won't have solved the problem but only prolonged it. If you receive a call from a troublemaker or some unpleasant intruder who will not take no for an answer, you will probably have to terminate the call very firmly, but even so, I'd recommend an even-tempered goodbye.

If you have, for some unexpected reason, to cut short a call *before* you want to, always apologize and arrange to phone again. Friends and business colleagues shouldn't have to ring you back when the ball is really in your court. It's a question of courtesy as well as phone bills.

However low we may be feeling, I think we should make a supreme effort to sound calm and pleasant. If we can manage to be cheerful when in fact we are depressed or unwell, it can actually make *us* feel better, as you may know from experience. And it will certainly make our friends feel better. There's a great deal to be said for good vibrations on the telephone lines.

Taking a message

The best phrase, I think, when you answer the phone for someone else, is: 'Who's calling, please?' (I'll never forget phoning a woman and getting her husband on the line; 'Who wants her?' he snapped, as if nobody could possibly want her!)

If you receive a call for someone who is out, ask if you can take a message, and if so write it down at once, with the name of the caller. If you don't catch the name, do ask to have it spelt. I think it's also wise to ask for a phone number in case the person wants to ring back at once. Never give away any personal facts about a friend to an unknown caller; you never know what complications may arise. If you are questioned, be calmly non-committal, and end the call with a pleasant, 'Thank you for ringing. I'll give her your message as soon as she gets back.' 'Thank you for calling' is a good way to end any telephone conversation. It has a warm, appreciative echo.

Duty calls

We all have to ring people from time to time when we don't really want to. Parents expect regular calls from their offspring (remember Maureen Lipman in the TV Telecom ad.?); husbands and wives often need reassuring that their partners have arrived safely, won't be late, etc. Information is required. Tender words are expected. Complaints abound. The demands of the telephone, where duty calls are concerned, can be arduous, and this is when we may see it as a tyrant. But if you can identify for a moment with the person who longs to hear from you, the task of phoning an over-demanding relative or partner will seem less problematic. We're all insecure in some way or another; we need to know that we are loved and thought about, and when someone is alone and anxious we really have to make an effort to cheer and comfort them for a few minutes, however inconvenient it may be. Never give a lonely person the feeling that he or she is a nuisance. Your call may mean more than you can ever imagine, and if they speak sharply or harangue you for neglect, that's probably just a sign of their inner turmoil.

For your own sake, as well as theirs, don't delay that duty call. 'Do it now!' is one of my favourite maxims and if I didn't try to live by it, this book would never have been ready for the publisher on time!

If you are on the receiving end of a duty call (and we have to be honest with ourselves about this!) it's a good idea to try and put yourself in the place of the person who is ringing you. Don't upbraid them, either openly or by implication. Nobody likes to be made to feel guilty and you will receive more calls, and longer ones, if you are a pleasure to talk to and don't carp or complain too much. A plaintive tone of voice is terribly off-putting. We all know this to be true but sometimes we don't quite hear ourselves as others hear us.

When you are making a difficult call, especially to an elderly person, you can sometimes make things easier if you concentrate on asking how they are, listening patiently, offering solace – and advice, if need be. Sometimes a lonely person needs only to off-load the pains and problems of the day into a sympathetic ear.

It's good to talk about your own activities, but do play down unhappy experiences and dreary details. Before you lift the receiver, think of something funny that's happened since last time you phoned, something that somebody said, a good radio or television programme, a bit of fascinating news you read in the paper. If the person has a rather dreary and uneventful lifestyle, don't upset them by going into rapturous details about your glamorous social life. Some people genuinely love to hear about their friends' successes and pleasures, others don't. You'll know which are which! Before you ring off be sure to say when you'll be likely to phone again or make a visit. Anyone who is lonely or depressed likes to have a definite time to look forward to. On the other hand, if *you* are the lonely one, it's best not to ask about the next call or complain if it doesn't come when it was promised; there are dozens of reasons why busy people can't get to a phone when they want to. Don't jump to the conclusion that you are forgotten, but if it turns out that you are, try to accept the fact, because there's nothing much you can do about it! Perhaps it's a mistake to rely too much on people who are not in sympathy with us.

Answerphones

The answerphone is obviously a must for those who are out a lot and depend on the telephone for their work. I'm not one of them, and I must confess that the first time I was greeted with that pre-recorded statement I hung up as soon as I heard the signal for me to start talking. With practice it became much easier (as most things do) although I once forgot to say who I was and had to ring back to apologize to the wretched thing. And isn't that the trouble? We think of it as a 'thing' rather than the valued possession of someone who will later listen to our message and phone us back. For a really satisfactory relationship of any kind, of course, we need some feedback, and for me it has always been a bit of a problem to talk to a machine that can't laugh at my jokes.

The best solution, for those who are unfamiliar with the situation, is to be prepared for an answerphone unless you are quite sure there won't be one. Think out your message in advance and possibly make a few notes so that you won't forget an important point. I find it useful to look at the whole thing through the eyes of someone who uses a machine of this kind every day. It must be quite intriguing to listen to the tape and hear what you've got!

If you use an answerphone yourself, make sure that your recorded instructions are not only clear but delivered in a particularly welcoming tone of voice. I like it when people say (as if they mean it) 'I'm sorry I can't be here to talk to you in person . . .', etc. Such an opening reminds you that you aren't really talking to a robot but to a live human being.

4

Writing to People

We all know the pleasure of receiving a letter from a friend, and there are few give-and-take exchanges more satisfying than a regular correspondence. If you find it difficult to express yourself in this way and would like to make your letters more lively and interesting, here are some tips to help you.

1. Don't worry too much about spelling or literary style; simply write as if you were talking. Imagine yourself chatting happily to your friend over a cup of tea and then discovering that someone had been making a tape recording of everything you said. A transcript of that tape would probably make a lovely letter – warm and uninhibited.

2. Some people like to make a rough draft and then revise it, cutting out the dull or repetitive bits, then copying it out. This is a good plan if you want to produce something special, but as a general rule I wouldn't recommend it because the result could sound stilted. The best personal letters are free and easy, cheerful and chatty, and reflect our own unique individuality.

3. Enclosures can make a letter particularly welcome – a pressed flower from the garden, a theatre programme, a newspaper cutting you know will interest your friend, or a clipping from a new wallpaper or curtain material. Photographs are always a delight and so are children's poems or drawings. My husband and I always put an enclosure in the envelope with the letter if we're separated, even if it's just a toffee paper or a leaf!

4. Never fill your letters with moans and dismal stories. This can be a temptation if you've been having a bad time and you know your correspondent will be sympathetic, but do

keep your grumbles to a minimum and try to see the funny side of your troubles. We all know people whose letters we dread because they always depress us. Read yours through very critically before you post it, to be sure you aren't putting a sheaf of misery into that envelope. It can be a great relief to get our troubles down on paper, and I think we ought to do it and do it with gusto. *But then we should burn the letter*! Afterwards we can sit down and write a more cheery one; it will seem much easier after unloading our sorrows and then destroying them. Matthew Manning, the well-known healer and hypnotherapist, suggests that we imagine writing down our worries on bits of paper, putting them onto a bonfire and watching the smoke carry them away into oblivion. It's a wonderful exercise in creative visualization and I think we can do much the same thing by writing a dismal – or angry – letter and then burning it.

5. There are times, of course, when we have to convey bad news or share our anxieties, but I don't think we should ever send a letter if we know it will cause *needless* unhappiness. Don't be falsely cheery but always lighten the gloom with something constructive and leave your reader with the thought of a courageous and positive person, not a dreary self-pitier.

6. Make sure that your handwriting is legible. If you find it quite impossible to write legibly, however hard you try, then perhaps it would be kinder to use a typewriter or write in block capitals. As you will know from being on the receiving end, it really is annoying and frustrating if you can't make out what your friend is saying to you without a prolonged decoding operation. It's quite a problem, I know, for many people; they can't even read their *own* writing!

'Thank you' letters

These days some people don't feel it's necessary to write thank you letters for presents and hospitality, and perhaps we shouldn't take these missives for granted or feel offended if we don't receive them. Nevertheless, it's a pleasing custom; most of us want to convey our appreciation, and a thank-you note can be very brief. It's always a pleasure for us to hear how much a friend liked the gift we sent, enjoyed the meal we cooked, etc. Chatty remarks such as: 'What a gorgeous supper that was! Congratulations!' Or: 'I loved every minute of our discussion/that video/the jam session'; or: 'Those new curtains of yours are fantastic!' means so much more than a mere, 'Thank you very much for an enjoyable evening'.

There are, of course, attractive 'thank-you' cards to buy and these are great, provided you scribble an individual comment inside. The personal touch is vital in all aspects of getting along with people and written messages are specially important because they are so often kept as souvenirs.

Holiday postcards

It's great fun to choose picture postcards that have a special significance for the recipient. For instance, in Crete I found a photograph of an ancient vase for a friend who makes pots, a harbour scene for a boating enthusiast, donkeys for a family with children, architectural remains for a historian. This may seem obvious but some people seem to grab a dozen identical cards, write the same message on them all and that's that! Everyone loves a postcard from an interesting location, whatever it depicts, but you can give added pleasure if you select your cards with care, and your friends will appreciate your thoughtfulness.

It isn't easy, on holiday, to think out a different message for every card, but the weather and your hotel should only occupy a line or two, leaving space for an individual comment such as: 'You'd adore this rugged scenery' or: 'The market is fascinating and I'm bringing you back a little present' or: 'I went to a Mozart concert last night and thought how much you'd have loved it . . .'. Just a little remark to show your friend or relative that you were thinking of her. If you are writing to someone you meet quite often, say when you are coming back and how much you are looking forward to seeing her again.

Letters to the bereaved

There is probably no more difficult letter to write than a message of consolation to someone who has just lost a beloved friend or relative. What on earth can one say? Surely words are totally inadequate to convey the sympathy we feel. And yet we have to pick up our pens and do our best. Some people find the task so daunting that they keep putting it off until they feel it is too late, and the letter is never sent. We must write at once; that's when our messages are most appreciated.

We can, of course, take the easy way out and buy a suitable card. This is quite acceptable if the bereaved is someone we don't know very well, but a letter is so much more appropriate for a person close to us, and I think we should make the effort. A personal message from the heart in one's own handwriting can mean a great deal to a friend in distress. And it's helpful to add a note at the end to say that no reply is necessary.

What, then, are the wisest and most helpful things to say? If I can do so with sincerity, I like to pay tribute to the one who has died, saying what a privilege it was to know her, and how much she will be missed. Pay tribute, too, to the character of the bereaved, knowing she will find the strength to carry on and gradually win her way back to a useful and satisfying life; most people find solace in the knowledge that their associates believe they have the courage to cope. However brief and simple your message may be, your friend will know you are thinking of her, and that's the most important thing.

When our son died, the most comforting of all the letters we

27

received was one that said, 'Be grateful for having had him'. Gratitude for happy memories is a deeply curative emotion after bereavement (or indeed at any time) and if you can awaken this idea in the mind of someone laid low by grief, as my friend did for me, you will be doing her a great service. Everyone needs a period of mourning, but a positive approach to the future is essential for a speedy recovery. When we have suffered a loss, we owe it to those around us, as well as to ourselves, to struggle back to normality – and even cheerfulness – as soon as we can. The support of our friends, including letters from those who can't be near us, is vital for this very difficult task.

When you write a letter of sympathy, you may like to offer practical help as well as loving thoughts. You could also send flowers, books or pictures – any little gift to show how you feel. A good novel can be wonderfully restorative; soon after we lost our son, I went back to *A Word Child* by Iris Murdoch, and I think it saved my sanity to identify with imaginary characters and suffer with them, instead of drowning in self-pity. The latest book by a favourite author could be the perfect choice. We must face the fact that grieving, although it is so necessary for recovery, has a lot to do with self-pity. This, of course, is the last thing we should say to someone recently bereaved, but it's a salutary thought, and I found it helpful when I was over the first few weeks.

Business letters

'What connection do business letters have with getting along with people?' you might ask. Quite a lot. A certain 'tone of voice' is apparent in letters of all kinds and even a formal communication can sound impatient or unfriendly if the writer is feeling that way and doesn't make a special effort to be amiable. The wrong tone can lose an order, delay a settlement or at least cause bad feeling. This doesn't mean, of course, that one should adopt a fawning attitude or fail to speak plainly when you have cause to do so. It simply means that 'a soft answer turneth away wrath', and that wrath is our natural enemy where good relationships are concerned.

A business letter, unlike a chatty, personal one, always has something specific to convey, and the writer must obviously avoid waffle and come to the point at once, expressing herself clearly and pleasantly, then signing off without more ado. A certain amount of planning may be necessary to get the facts in the right order and to avoid superfluous wordage and repetition. Be very careful to avoid any possibility of confusion. Business letters are an important factor in getting along with people, whether it be the gas board, a building inspector, school governor, tax man or whoever. Don't be intimidated by bureaucracy. The people in these offices are all human beings with their own problems to cope with, and they will warm to a pleasant approach just as you would yourself. Write in a natural and simple style, avoiding stilted phrases such as 'I am in receipt of your letter of the 15th inst.' This is not the modern way.

Send off replies as soon as possible and apologize for any unavoidable delay. Thank your correspondent for any previous letter and check that you have answered all queries, asked for clarification or whatever may be necessary. If you have made a mistake, don't try to cover it up. Say you are sorry, put it right and don't feel guilty about it. We all make mistakes and so long as you are honest and straightforward about them, they are usually forgotten very quickly.

Don't use scented, coloured or fussily decorated writing paper for business letters! If you have no headed paper, use plain white sheets with matching envelopes. It's best to type such letters but if this is impossible, be sure to write legibly. Your address, telephone number and the date should appear in the top right-hand corner, with the reference number a couple of lines lower down, preceded by 'Your ref:'. Then a little lower down still, but on the left, the name and address of the recipient. The first line of the address may be the name of the individual, if you know who it is, or somebody's job title or the name of the firm. Start the letter with 'Dear Mr/Mrs/

Miss/Ms So-and-So' if you know the name, otherwise 'Dear Sir', 'Dear Madam' or 'Dear Sir/Madam'. I would always recommend addressing your letter to the individual concerned, if possible, to give it that friendly personal touch. You don't need to have had a regular correspondence with them or any previous dealings at all – you may just have found out the name by making a quick phone call to the firm's switchboard. You could refer to a trade journal or directory but this may be misleading because people are constantly changing their jobs; you obviously don't want to address your letter to someone who has left the firm.

Don't indent your paragraphs, and do leave a space between them. Don't forget to quote the date and reference number of the last letter you received and any subject heading which may be required to facilitate filing. End your letter with 'Yours faithfully' (never 'truly') when you start with 'Dear Sir (or Madam)' or 'Yours sincerely' when you begin 'Dear Mr/Mrs/Ms So-and-So'. If you have met or have corresponded frequently, you could precede it with 'Best wishes' or 'Kind regards'.

Finally, check that you have not forgotten any necessary enclosures such as a cheque or photocopy and that you have put the letter in the right envelope!

Letters to journals

Letters of complaint (or praise) to newspapers and magazines are a valuable form of self-expression. Here you can vent your anger or delight, speaking not only for yourself but probably for hundreds of others as well.

If you have cause for complaint about some local or national issue, it is so much more useful to write a letter about it than merely to blow your top to your friends. Action is often taken as a result of letters, especially if a large number of people write about the same matter. So why not make the effort to put your views on paper next time you feel angry about some injustice? It will not only help to get the anger out of your system, but also give satisfaction, if your letter is published, to those who share your views but don't feel able to write.

The secret of a good letter to a journal is to keep it brief and to the point. Give it a 'shape' – a beginning, middle and end – so that you open with a pithy sentence which states the problem, follow with a short development of your protest and end with your proposed remedy.

For example, a letter to the local newspaper, addressed to the editor, may run something like this.

Dear Sir,

Yesterday I had to stand outside in a sudden cloudburst at the bus stop opposite the Fox and Pelican in Grayshott, waiting for the 268 to Aldershot. The bus was very late and I was soaked to the skin. A frail old lady with a stick was waiting with me and could easily have caught her death of cold. There isn't even a seat!

I understand that the bus shelter there was vandalized some time ago and that there are no plans to replace it, but if something isn't done before the winter sets in there could be serious consequences.

Yours faithfully,

Dianne Doubtfire

This is a genuine complaint and, if others write in a similar vein, some action may well result. In any case, we have the satisfaction of knowing we did something about it. (Note: a shelter has now been built!)

I'm also a great believer in letters of praise; a word of appreciation for an outstanding performance in a concert or play, an act of kindness, or a particularly good article or short story in a magazine can give great pleasure. We may often think of sending such a letter but never get round to it. The best thing is to write it at once and mail it the same day.

Letters will be redirected from theatres, radio or TV channels, magazine editors and publishers if you mark the envelope 'Personal. Please forward'.

There are other ways, of course, in which the written word can give pleasure and comfort. Stationers today carry vast arrays of greetings cards in attractive designs to suit all tastes and all situations, from 'I love you' and 'Get well soon' to 'Bon voyage' and 'Sorry I forgot your birthday'. Some are dazzlingly beautiful, some so funny that you burst out laughing when you open them up and read the punchline. Some cards are blank inside for you to add your own special message. When we are separated from those we are fond of, the written word, in whatever form, can keep us in touch and remind them that they are not forgotten. I have many friends I only hear from at Christmas, but just a scribble inside the card warms my heart –as I hope my little note warms theirs – and sometimes such a contact, which only takes a minute, can lead to a letter, a phone call or a meeting.

I know that greetings cards are quite expensive, especially those with reproductions of famous paintings, but the pleasure they give is out of all proportion to the price. They are often preserved as lasting reminders of somebody's loving thoughts, a storehouse of delight to browse through at times of boredom and depression.

Perhaps there is someone you could pen a little note to this very day – someone who would rejoice to see your writing on the envelope. Why not give it a thought and do it before you forget?

5

Different Ages and Backgrounds

Children

Talking to children and playing games with them is one of the most rewarding of human relationships. If we can get it right, it's full of fun and surprises for us, as well as for them; their innocence is a constant delight and I am always amazed by their instinctive perception and subtle appreciation of facts and ideas that one might think would be beyond their comprehension.

Anyone who has taught in a school knows all too well the pains and pleasures of dealing with young people, but those who have never had much to do with them often find it daunting – and even frightening – to be obliged to spend time alone with a child. They feel they have no point of contact and are afraid of failure. In fact there are many ways of getting along with children if we can only put aside our apprehensions and try to remember how we felt about grown-ups when we were their age. To establish rapport with people of all ages we must try to put ourselves in their place, to imagine what it's like to be in their shoes. This leads to the kind of empathy that inspires confidence, and it's especially important when we are dealing with children. We can all remember those boring or unsympathetic adults who towered above us, patronized us and always seemed to want to get away as quickly as possible, back to their own kind. To be a success with children we must obviously do our best to avoid that kind of distancing. 'Let's play a game!' will nearly always get a good response if we show that we are willing to play on *their* terms, not ours. Give them the feeling that you are enjoying yourself, even if you aren't. Do what *they* want to do (within reason!) and don't be critical. Try to enter into the spirit of the game, being prepared to make mistakes, make a fool of yourself and laugh a lot. It's marvellous when, sometimes quite unexpectedly, we can really enjoy ourselves, joining their world and extending our own horizons.

We should never underestimate the immense importance of children's relationships with adults. Their introduction to life –and often their whole future – hangs on the way they feel about us when they are small. We can foster rebellion, anger and frustration or we can give them contentment and the daily joy of new discoveries. Whether we are dealing with our own children or other people's we must surely do all we can to offer comfort, information and encouragement.

If you find it difficult to get along with children, here are a few suggestions.

The games and amusements we choose will obviously depend very much on the age of the child, but they will also depend on interests, intelligence and temperament. Most youngsters enjoy some kind of participation. When you are reading from a story book, for instance, don't forget to show the child the illustrations, pausing to discuss the characters, to repeat any specially intriguing paragraphs, to ask questions. ('What do you think is going to happen next?') Encourage the listener to become involved in the story, to identify with the hero, to imagine the setting.

Most children love drawing, even from a very early age, and if you arm yourself with a note pad and pencil, you will find you can easily engage your young friend in making pictures. For children under five, you could start by drawing a rectangle. 'What's it going to be?' you say. 'Is it a house – or a car – or a ship – or a horse. . . ?' the child will probably decide at once, adding windows, wheels, funnels, legs or whatever. If not, you can make a start yourself and then hand over the pencil. Older children will usually enjoy producing detailed drawings and all you have to do is watch.

And, of course, there is the age-old art of conversation, which should surely be encouraged in children of all ages. We must relate to them on their own level but never preaching or patronizing. Ask them about their hobbies, their pets, their toys. You could also talk to them about their problems. Adults are inclined to forget that children have problems, too – anxiety about their lessons, their health, their parents, fears of other children, not to mention the thousand-and-one dangers of everyday life which they see on television and read about in the papers.

You will get along with children better if you don't ask them stereotyped questions such as 'When do you go back to school?' or 'What's your favourite subject?' A better start might be 'What's your favourite animal?' or 'Who's your favourite pop star?'

When you are playing with children don't be tempted to play your *own* game. I was once in charge of a small girl with a really splendid doll's house, and she burst into tears when I began to rearrange the furniture! On another occasion I made the mistake of winding up a clockwork car for a little boy when he wanted to do it himself. Children have very definite ideas about how they want things done. This is the kind of character and initiative we admire and it shouldn't be suppressed simply because we think it is misguided. We should point out their faults in such a way that they do not feel discouraged; if they are punished or humiliated for making mistakes they become inhibited and resist experiment. In later life they may be shy and lacking in self-esteem, feeling guilty about their mistakes instead of seeing them as part of the process of learning. When I'm writing a book I have to keep reminding myself that 'trial and error are part of the task' or else I might feel frustrated by all the rewriting I have to do.

You could teach any child of a suitable age to play Scrabble, Patience, chess or any of a dozen well-loved family games they haven't come across. And of course the public library will have books on all manner of ways of amusing children, from puzzles and quizzes to paper sculpture and model-making.

Television, whether we approve or not, gives a great deal of pleasure to many youngsters. If you ask them about their favourite programmes, watch with them (if they want you to), and introduce them to some of your own that have universal appeal, you will create a splendid foundation of common interests. You may, of course, disapprove most heartily of some of the programmes that delight your young friends, but if you show it you will forfeit their esteem at a stroke! Adults are much the same; if someone denigrates a TV programme, book or film that we have enjoyed, we are bound to feel a little dashed and a little less eager to share our views in future. 'Tell me why you like it' is a wise response to a child and may lead to a better understanding. We must be prepared to *listen* with patience and sympathy if we are to win the affection and respect we need for happy relationships.

I think it's important not to force our company on children who don't really want it. 'Come and play with Auntie, dear!' brings back painful memories of my own childhood when I was busy with some lone activity and only wanted to be left in peace.

The generation gap

I don't attach much importance to people's ages in years; it's their attitudes that really matter. Wisdom often grows with maturity but we know this isn't always true; young people may surpass their elders in perception if not in factual knowledge. The trouble is that elderly people, simply on account of their age, sometimes take for granted respect they do not really merit. Conversely, youngsters may feel needlessly inadequate just because they lack experience. My advice, therefore, is to think as little as possible about people's ages, apart from giving due consideration to any health problems an elderly person may have. Try to relate to everyone on an equal footing so that the difference in your ages dwindles into insignificance.

I'd like to quote an anonymous text entitled 'So Long Are You Young' which hangs in our hall and enchants our guests.

Youth is not a time of life – it is a state of mind. It is not a matter of ripe cheeks, red lips and supple knees; it is a temper of the will, a quality of the imagination, a vigour of the emotions: it is a freshness of the deep springs of life.

Youth means a temperamental predominance of courage over timidity, of the appetite for adventure over love of ease. This often exists in a man of fifty more than in a boy of twenty. Nobody grows old by living a number of years; people grow old only be deserting their ideals. Years wrinkle the skin, but to give up enthusiasm wrinkles the soul. Worry, doubt, self-distrust, fear and despair – these are the long, long years that bow the head and turn the growing spirit back to dust.

Whether seventy or seventeen, there is in every being's mind the love of wonder, the sweet amazement at the stars and the star-like things and thoughts, the undaunted challenge of events, the unfailing childlike appetite for what next, and the joy in the game of life. You are as young as your faith, as old as your doubt, as young as your self-confidence, as old as your fear, as young as your hope, as old as your despair.

In the central place of your mind there is a wireless station. So long as it receives messages of beauty, hope, cheer, courage, grandeur and power from the earth, from men and from the infinite, so long are you young.

If we can keep these thoughts in mind, the people around us will recognize the signs of a positive approach to life and feel more at ease with us.

Different generations have always disagreed about small matters as well as fundamentals and the sooner we agree to 'live and let live', the sooner we shall overcome the friction and misery these differences can cause. The arguments between parents and their sons and daughters obviously top the list where acrimony between age-groups is concerned, and because older people have responsibility for their offspring it's up to them, I feel, to make every effort to understand the attitudes of the young even if they disagree with them. Older people may show more tolerance than those who are immature and ablaze with the rebellious impulses that are natural to them. Idealism, although sometimes misguided, should inspire the admiration and respect of those who, in their later years, have come to adopt a more practical approach. If we are to get along with people younger than ourselves we should never condemn them for their high principles even though we may disapprove of their methods.

Some folk feel ill at ease with younger people out of a mistaken sense of inferiority. Fading looks, poor health or reduced circumstances can make them look at those who are young, healthy, beautiful and successful with jaundiced eyes instead of the affection and admiration they probably deserve.

Middle-aged people often disapprove of the young – their clothes, hairstyles, off-hand behaviour and general attitudes – in which case they feel irritated and resentful. They may also feel self-conscious in case they are considered stuffy and narrow-minded; even when we disapprove of someone we usually want to be liked and respected by them, sometimes forgetting that we ourselves may give rise to criticism.

Young people, of course, may have difficulty in relating to their elders, and often lack the experience they need to handle the situation wisely. We can all become so deeply involved in our own lives that we overlook the problems of those around us.

Alex, aged twenty, living at home with his widowed mother, was so concerned about the danger of losing his job that he was quite unaware that his mother was suffering from multiple sclerosis. She hadn't told him, not wanting to upset him, and he had been complaining because she often spoke sharply to him and seemed unwilling to prepare elaborate meals for him and his girl friend. It wasn't until his aunt told him the truth that sympathy and understanding took the place of acrimony.

Deirdre, in her fifties, suspected that her husband was in love with a younger woman and was so distressed that she did not realize her daughter was sharing a flat with a man who gambled away his wages and drank too much. When Deirdre's husband finally left her, her daughter returned home and the two of them cried on each other's shoulders and eventually came to terms with a new life.

Most of these problems, serious as they are, could be greatly relieved, if not solved, by a greater degree of honesty and communication across the generation gap – in both directions. The young should try to confide in their elders, the middle-aged to discuss their anxieties with their sons and daughters. In most cases, this kind of honesty would be welcomed. Anyone who admits to unhappiness and asks for advice is bestowing trust, and that trust is usually respected. The confession of distress and the admission of guilt can lead to a closer understanding and encourage honesty in return. In a later chapter we shall consider difficult relationships in greater detail.

We all need to feel relaxed and natural if we are to be happy, but being our true selves will, on occasion, upset those who don't see eye to eye with us. What can we do about that? 'To thine own self be true' is another fine ideal, but being our true selves is only desirable if we are to be our true *best* selves, otherwise we could find excuses for all kinds of questionable behaviour. 'Oh, I always sit like that', said a young man when I complained about him spreading his long legs out in front of him so that everyone had to make a detour or fall over them. A woman who never shut a door without banging it said, 'I can't help it – it's just me!' Sometimes we may flaunt our transgressions because they give us an air of devil-may-care and lift us out of the ordinary. I've been guilty of that myself – and still am from time to time.

It isn't only different ages and backgrounds we have to consider: it's different temperaments, as well. Some people like a good argument, some are upset by any kind of strong discussion. Being too outspoken (especially after a drink too many) can make one very unpopular. I've always argued in favour of honesty whenever possible but sometimes I've overstepped the mark and regretted it. We must watch out for any vulnerable spots and respect them, just as we hope that others will respect ours. Everyone finds certain subjects distressing and our ability to discern these areas and avoid causing pain, will have an important bearing on our ability to get along with people. If we can look on others as fellow human beings, whatever their ages, with weaknesses and virtues, just as we have ourselves, then there is no reason why such differences should impair our relationships.

Foreigners

Getting along with people from other countries can present difficulties merely from the language point of view, but if there is also prejudice on either side ('Those Blacks! Those Germans! Those Brits!'), the problem is far more serious. People are no longer being judged on their merits but discriminated against purely on account of their origins.

The more I have travelled, the more firmly convinced I have become that people of all nations are fundamentally alike; the human need for love, laughter, health, food, shelter – and peace of mind – is universal. You have only to watch little children in a nursery school where many nationalities play happily together to realize that the problems arise from prejudice that is instilled by other people – family and friends, the media, and sometimes by foreigners themselves in their attitudes to us. What, then, can we do to improve the situation?

Let's first of all be honest with ourselves, facing up to any prejudice caused by our upbringing, reminding ourselves that all prejudices (prejudgements) are damaging and unjust, and that we ourselves would not wish to be on the receiving end of any such discrimination. In my view, individuals from all nations and backgrounds are good and acceptable unless proved otherwise.

Language will always be a barrier for those of us who are not linguists. It's a great advantage to learn a few words and phrases in a foreign country, but most of us have to use gestures, diagrams and a dictionary for communication. Many years ago I was on a day trip to Cologne while I was staying in Belgium. I lost my way back to the railway station, didn't know a word of German and couldn't find anyone who spoke English or French. At last I resorted to imitating a railway engine like a four-year-old, with the appropriate noises! It worked like magic. An elderly man laughingly sketched a little street plan on an old envelope and pointed me in the right direction.

Many people have an inbuilt suspicion of those from abroad, especially if their skins happen to be of a different colour. The sooner we can accept the fact that there are good, bad and middling folk the world over, the sooner we can enjoy the company of foreigners, giving and taking in friendly comradeship.

The class problem

Most of us understand that but for a trick of fate we could easily have been born into a different environment, one that bestowed more privileges than we now enjoy, or a great deal fewer. 'There but for the grace of God go I' is a thought that opens our hearts to deeper understanding when we are confronted with people who behave badly on account of their disadvantaged background. I would not argue that all bad behaviour stems from misfortune but I'd say that 90% of it does. Those who have experienced injustice, cruelty or deprivation are far more likely to suffer the kind of resentful and rebellious feelings that can so easily lead to rudeness, intolerance or crime.

This may or may not relate to class differences but poverty and lack of opportunity is obviously more common among working class people and, although I hate the very word 'class', we cannot avoid its implications when we are trying to

41

get along with people in Britain today. We have to face the fact that we live in a divisive society, one in which a 'top-drawer' accent or a university education are an advantage when it comes to employment and promotion, one in which 'good breeding', knowledge of etiquette, smart clothes, expensive cars and large homes win respect from some and scorn from others, quite irrespective of the character of the person concerned.

This is why, when those from very different backgrounds wish to relate happily to one another, the problems cannot be overlooked. The company director can have a perfectly amicable relationship with the plumber who comes to mend a burst pipe – and vice versa – but if the two were to meet at a dinner party (which isn't likely) they could both be ill at ease. This saddens me. Most people are relaxed and comfortable with those from a similar background, and make very little effort to mix outside their own circle. Writers, artists, musicians, actors and others engaged in the arts usually attain a kind of no-man's-land by means of professional achievement and are quite happy in any company. If they use the wrong knife, wear the wrong clothes or, like Eliza Dolittle, come out with unsuitable expressions, it doesn't really bother them.

So, what am I trying to say about the class problem? I have to admit that getting along with someone at the opposite end of the social scale, whether higher or lower, is very difficult for many people and can only be achieved by those who respect every individual, regardless of background. It isn't always easy, but I'm sure it's an ideal worth striving for.

When I lived on the Isle of Wight, I was invited to Parkhurst Prison to give talks on Creative Writing to an audience of longterm convicts, some of them lifers. No warder was in the room (although I'm sure there must have been someone standing by in case of trouble) but I was surprised to feel no anxiety once I began to address them. They were interested in what I had to say. They asked questions. They laughed. And when they filed out at the end, each one shook me by the hand

and thanked me for coming. We had found common ground. This is the secret of all good communication and we can manage it with almost anyone if we can overcome our apprehensions and make the effort.

6

Visitors

The custom of visiting people in their homes and inviting them to our own is worldwide and delightful; it must have been going on for millions of years. Can't you imagine people sitting in one another's caves, talking about their children and their parents and what they had for dinner, and making arrangements for return visits? They must have taken little presents, just as we do today, and admired each other's pot roasts and wall paintings and skin rugs.

Giving and accepting hospitality is certainly one of life's greatest pleasures, but there are some hazards we need to consider if we are to escape the attendant stress as far as possible. One could argue that it is a mistake to invite people to your home unless you like them, but for family or business reasons – or simply out of compassion – it is sometimes necessary to do so. Entertaining people who are not on our wavelength (or being entertained by them) is a delicate operation but the problem must be carefully considered if we are to manage these exchanges wisely, causing the least possible strain to ourselves and everyone concerned.

You may not relish the visit of a carping, irritable relative or an arrogant colleague, but when the situation is unavoidable there is nothing you can do but make the best of it, smooth things over if they threaten to become problematic, temper over-heated discussions as soon as they arise and guide the conversation into a less threatening area. As the host or hostess, it's up to you to preserve a friendly atmosphere if you possibly can, although on some occasions a modicum of conflict might clear the air.

I have found that the most beneficial approach is to assure myself that I don't *have* to be upset by anybody else's unpleasantness; *it's entirely up to me how I react.* Easier said than done, I know, but with practice we can learn to relax away our resentment and maintain our own 'still centre'. This is not only essential for our happiness but also for our health. Nervous tension can be very damaging and many people simply do not realize that it is in their power to overcome it (see chapter 9).

The happiest visits, of course, are those to and from the friends and relations we love very dearly and genuinely want to be with. And yet, as we all know from bitter experience, when we are very fond of someone it's all too easy to become emotional over issues that would not trouble us if we *didn't* care so much. By over-reacting we bring about the very friction we dread. The best advice I can offer, based on over half a century of mistakes, remorse and gradual improvement, is to 'do unto others as you would have them do unto you'. It's a good old maxim that never fails if you apply it with honesty and compassion. If we put ourselves in the other person's place we can see things in a more balanced way and monitor our reactions. When we fail – as from time to time we are bound to – the first thing, surely, is to recognize the fault, apologize and put the matter right as soon as possible. Where affection exists on both sides, the relationship often becomes even warmer and deeper as a result. We must try to be honest with ourselves as well as with others, so that the danger of conflict can be arrested at the outset.

And now let's consider, on a more domestic level, how visits to and from our friends can be made to run even more smoothly. You won't agree with all my suggestions but I hope that some of them will be helpful.

Do's and don'ts: the weekend guest

- Do let your hostess know in good time when you expect to arrive and depart. She will need to know how many meals to prepare.
- Do say in advance if you have any particular dislikes with regard to food. I once made a splendid casserole only to discover, when it was on the table, that one of my guests couldn't eat onions.

- Do confirm your visit the day before to avoid any mistake about dates and times.
- Do take warm clothes in case their heating isn't very effective, a book to read in bed and any medications you may need.
- Do take a small gift, including something extra if there are children. An unusual jig-saw puzzle, a constructional toy or a fascinating book, according to age and interests, can make a weekend more peaceful for everyone. I'll never forget the 'friend' who brought our small son a trumpet!
- Do check your bedding in good time in case you need extra blankets or pillows.
- Do offer to help in the kitchen but don't insist if your hostess prefers you to relax.
- Do confess if you break something. Offer to replace it, and if she won't accept, send a little present afterwards to make amends.
- Do strip your bed and fold the sheets before you leave unless your hostess employs someone who looks after such things.
- Do write a warm, appreciative thank you letter without delay.

- Don't arrive early. Your hostess might be hoovering the hall, varnishing her nails or doing any of a hundred last minute jobs.
- Don't moan about your journey.
- Don't talk about anything distressing at meal-times; it's bad for the digestion and spoils everybody's enjoyment of the food.
- Don't drink so much that you become over-talkative or quarrelsome.
- Don't light a cigarette, pipe or cigar without asking permission. Many people have health problems with regard to smoke, quite apart from disliking the fumes and the smell that lingers in the curtains!
- Don't make unnecessary noise before your hostess gets up in the morning or after she has gone to bed.

- Don't leave anything behind!

Do's and don'ts: the host or hostess

- Do switch off the radio or television as soon as you hear the doorbell, and welcome your guest at the front door.
- Do offer tea, coffee or a drink on arrival. If it's a drink, say what's on offer unless you've got most things.
- Do remember to put white wine in the fridge at least an hour before the meal.
- Do keep calm and cheerful, no matter what goes wrong. A panicky hostess upsets everybody and you'll cope so much better if you don't get flustered.
- Do give your guests the chance to be alone for a while if they are staying for a weekend. People often like to go for a lone walk, for instance, in a strange environment.
- Do make it easy for your guest to go to bed early or lie in late. Ask what time they'd like a cup of tea, or preferably provide tea-making equipment in the bedroom.
- Do ask if there are any TV programmes they specially want to see. I remember inviting a friend for the weekend, before knowing it was the Wimbledon Tennis Final. I hardly dared to ask if she was interested, but I'm glad I did because she was as keen as I was. 'I thought you'd never ask!' she said. The weekend was an enormous success; we watched the tennis for seven solid hours, with meals on our laps!
- Do be understanding if your guest doesn't go much on your dogs/cats/offspring. We all know that animals and children can dominate any gathering if they are allowed to. Take care that yours don't steal the show!
- Do get ready to receive your guests in good time. Rushing causes nervous tension and upsets both you and your friends. Decide in good time what you are going to wear, make yourself look good and then forget about it, concentrating all your attention on your visitors.
- Do put a carafe of water and a glass in the bedroom, in case your guest wants to take a pill or is thirsty in the night.

- Do provide a portable radio if possible; some people can't bear to miss the news.

- Don't pile a guest's plate with everything that's going. Serve in separate dishes so that a small eater can choose how much to take.
- Don't make your guest feel guilty if she arrives late.
- Don't let radio, discs or television over-ride conversation, unless your visitor requests it.
- Don't denigrate your partner in front of guests; it's embarrassing for everyone.
- Don't hesitate to deny permission to smoke. I think it's quite reasonable to say, pleasantly but firmly: 'I'm very sorry, but I'd really rather you didn't'. It's an extremely difficult problem: if somebody smokes just one cigarette it can ruin a party for a non-smoker with a chest infection or eye-trouble, and yet for an addict it's hell to be deprived (see page 57).

Finally, I don't think we should ever allow differences of class or affluence to interfere with the giving and taking of hospitality. Whether you are rich or poor or neither, true friendship will always transcend such artificial barriers if it is allowed to do so. A sandwich and a cup of tea in a small shabby room becomes a feast when two people who like one another are laughing and talking together, just as a sumptuous meal in a luxurious dining room has no savour without the warmth of good companionship. We should feel no shame on account of our simple fare and humble surroundings, nor envy of those more comfortably placed than ourselves. Neither should we try to impress others, if fortune has smiled upon us. Let's forget about success and social standing, only concerning ourselves with helping one another and giving pleasure, no matter on which side of the 'fence' we find ourselves. Fences change, but affection and mutual respect can never change if those concerned have got their values right.

Hospital visits

Visiting time means a great deal to those in hospital as most of us know, either through personal experience or through friends and relatives. When you visit someone, do try to be punctual. She is probably watching the door, eager to see a familiar face among the influx of strangers. Wear cheerful clothes and a cheerful smile, and take a gift, however small – something to bring comfort when visiting time is over and the patient is alone again.

Try to find something that will help to pass the lonely hours more pleasantly, possibly something related to her special interests. It could be books, magazines, games, puzzles, writing paper and envelopes (ready stamped), drawing book or notebook with pencils and rubber, a potted plant, fruit juice or the proverbial grapes. Ask what she would like you to take next time (and don't take 'Oh no, nothing, thanks!' for an answer). A person who is sick might be short of ideas but pleased to accept your suggestions. Find out what books you might buy or borrow from the library, what extra items of food are permissible. A woman might like toilet water, luxury soap, make-up, or perhaps some embroidery or knitting to work on. Most people would welcome a packet of thin sandwiches – ham, chicken or smoked salmon, for instance. It would often be greatly appreciated if you could offer to do some laundry.

Ask how the patient is feeling and listen sympathetically but do your best to sound cheerful, and don't encourage morbid speculation. A positive mental attitude is vitally important to recovery, whatever the complaint. Needless to say, *never* tell *anyone* they look awful!

When your visit unexpectedly coincides with someone else's, be sure that you neither intrude on a sentimental meeting nor insist on leaving when in fact you would be welcome to stay. And when the visiting time is over, say what day you'll be coming again, if this is possible. Time goes slowly in hospital and it's good to have pleasures to look forward to.

7

Difficult Relationships

I could write a whole book on this one subject, but I'll do my best to offer some useful guidelines for dealing with the personal problems that beset us all from time to time. We have to face the fact that some people are so persistently offensive that we should, if possible, phase them out of our lives. It is only when we are compelled to live or work with difficult people, or when they need our help, that we must make a supreme effort to reach some kind of rapport.

It seems to me that honest communication is at the heart of all good relationships. How else can we reach mutual understanding and find common ground?

In Paul Scott's novel, *Staying On*, Judy Tusker has this to say:

> 'Tusker and I do not truly communicate with one another any more,' she told the empty living room. 'His silence is his silence and my loquacity is my loquacity but they amount to the same thing. I can't hear what he is thinking and he does not hear what I am saying. So we are cut off from one another, living separate lives under the same roof. Perhaps this is how it has always been between us but only became apparent in our old age.'

Many people find communication very difficult. They may be suffering from inhibitions bred in childhood, or are afraid that conversation will force them to reveal a hidden secret or probe a painful area of their lives; some cannot find the words to express themselves and feel ashamed of the fact; some feel out of their depth with people they think of as better educated or wiser than they are; others just prefer to keep themselves to themselves, content in their own private worlds. An understanding of the reasons can help us to make contact with

50

people who will not or cannot communicate. It may be that we ourselves, unknowingly, are blocking the friendly give-and-take we long for. Sometimes it's possible to break the deadlock by saying gently, 'What's wrong? Can't you tell me about it?' Such an honest but caring approach may prompt a reply that contains the apology or confession the other person has very much wanted to make. (In such cases we must beware of intruding on the confidence by asking too many questions or bringing up the subject later. If a woman has admitted that her husband beats her she doesn't want to be asked about it next time she sees her confidante!) If we cannot, by persuasion or sympathy, create the rapport we need for a good relationship there may be nothing to do but get on with our own lives and hope that time may bring about an improvement in the situation.

Some time ago I had a wonderful phone call from a friend who had refused to talk about a disagreement that was keeping us apart. 'I was wrong,' she said, in tears. 'I've just heard a radio programme and I see I was wrong. Let's meet and talk it through.' We did, and in ten minutes we both realized that we had misunderstood each other. Our friendship is now stronger and warmer than ever before.

Some relationships, however, are so difficult and dangerous that they are outside the scope of this book and require professional advice. For instance, I know of a married couple who never speak to one another, a man who banished his son from home when he discovered he was gay, and a woman who took to heroin because her senile mother was making her life intolerable. Such tragic problems as these are far more common than is generally realized. Professional help should always be sought in such cases, but an emergency lifeline may be a call to the Samaritans; it can be a great relief to phone them and unburden oneself to a sympathetic and patient listener. I know, because I've done it myself.

Getting along with people, in general terms, wouldn't present too many problems if everyone (including oneself) were consistently good-humoured and forgiving. As things are, even the most well-balanced person can, at times, be totally unreasonable, and some folk seem to be unreasonable most of the time. These, of course, are the ones who present the greatest challenge – the ones who always have to be right, who lack consideration, who will not listen. To manage our personal relationships wisely and well, we have to consider very carefully how best to deal with those who appear to enjoy making life difficult for themselves and everyone else.

First of all, let's consider *why* people are greedy, selfish, envious or vindictive. A difficult background, heredity, ill-treatment or any manner of frustrated ambition or traumatic experience can produce the kind of personality we find so hard to cope with. Although we must try to understand the reasons behind the bad behaviour we encounter, whether it be from relatives, friends or strangers, understanding and sympathy may not be enough to ease the situation. If a woman in the office where you work is constantly ill-tempered, lazy and disruptive, it won't help very much to learn that her father is an alcoholic and her husband has deserted her. The problem remains, but if you can make her feel acceptable, she may improve. People who behave badly dislike themselves. They behave badly *because* they dislike themselves, and then they dislike themselves even more! They feel unwanted and rejected, and they very much need a sympathetic friend. If you can be that friend, you will do a great service to the person in question, to yourself and to everyone around. My advice, therefore, when people are disruptive is to do all we can to help them, comfort them and restore the balance. Sometimes we are so distraught by their behaviour that we add to the tension rather than diminish it. For our own sakes, as well as theirs, we must try to take the heat out of every critical situation.

If our efforts fail, perhaps we have unwittingly appeared pious, self-opinionated or intrusive. It isn't easy to strike the right note when someone is out of temper; our own tempers are sometimes frayed as well! And if you don't know the person very well you may not be able to gauge the response.

We all have different needs when we are upset. Some want loving-kindness, some to be left alone (yet knowing they are not out of favour), others respond remarkably well to a bit of straight talking ('Come on, Kate, I know you've had a raw deal but it's time you stopped grizzling and got some work done. How about finishing those letters before lunch?'). Many people welcome a philosophical talk but others resent any suggestion of a positive approach, taking it, perhaps, as a personal criticism. Whatever line you take, I suggest you try to remain as calm and relaxed as possible.

I'd like to quote here from Dr Maxwell Maltz, the renowned plastic surgeon. This is taken from his book *Psycho-Cybernetics*, which has helped thousands of troubled people to solve their problems.

It is our own responses that we have to be concerned about – not other people's. We can tighten up, become angry, anxious or resentful and 'feel hurt'. Or, we can make no response, remain relaxed and feel no hurt. Scientific experiments have shown that it is impossible to feel fear, anger, anxiety or negative emotions of any kind while the muscles of the body are kept perfectly relaxed . . . You alone are responsible for your responses and reactions. You do not *have* to respond at all. You can remain relaxed and free from injury.

A calm state of mind is certainly essential if we are to get along with difficult people comfortably and avoid needless friction. 'But surely we have to let off steam sometimes?' you may be thinking. And of course you're right. It's a mistake to suppress our anger to such an extent that it simmers below the surface and then explodes without warning; we all need a safety valve. Most of the time, however, we can learn to 'let it ride', to allow the irritations of the day to run off our shoulders 'like water off a duck's back'. When I'm provoked and tempted to react unwisely, I often think to myself: 'Calm down! Duck's back!' More often than not, it works, and I'm free to use my energy for creative projects instead of useless argument.

Is the problem yours or theirs?

We often spoil our relationships by taking unnecessary responsibility for problems which belong to someone else. In his book *All in the Mind?*, Dr Brian Roet says that we must be sure there really is a problem and if so, *who* has the problem. He goes on to say that the first step is to ask yourself questions such as: 'What does it mean to me? How does it feel? What limits my dealing with it? What role does my attitude play?' When I asked myself those questions in relation to a dilemma that faced me recently, I realized that it didn't really mean as much to me as I thought it did. My pride was hurt, that was all. Once I realized this, and understood that the problem was not really mine but someone else's, I was suddenly free of the pressure.

Dr Roet goes on to say that some people complain about situations that are unchangeable facts of life. These are not 'matters difficult of solution', but situations that are inevitable and unresponsive to change. Parents, for example, complain about the 'problems' they have with their teenage children and sometimes they are driven to seek professional advice. They complain that their children do not tidy their rooms, dress properly, are late for meals, are not polite to adults, stay out late, and so on.

Once these are seen as problems, much time, energy and emotion is spent trying to resolve them. Hours are spent in discussion, worry, reasoning, bribery, punishment, all to solve a problem which may be a natural phenomenon of growing up. The sleepless nights and grey hairs, as a rule have no marked effect on the behaviour of the teenagers involved.

Here is an example of somebody else's problem eroding

54

our happiness: Jeremy is married to a beautiful but unfaithful woman who is persistently unkind to him. He loves her deeply and does not want a separation because he believes she will change. Shirley, his mother, was allowing the situation to destroy her happiness: she was living Jeremy's life, not her own, although there was nothing she could do to solve his problem. Sometimes we have to accept the fact that people we love are enmeshed in miseries we cannot alleviate. Our love and concern will naturally be a comfort, but I think it's a grave mistake to surrender the quality – and often the usefulness – of our lives on account of other people's problems that are beyond our control. In Shirley's case she was not only spoiling her own life but her husband's as well. 'Try to put it out of your mind – there's nothing we can do', he pleaded. 'I *can't*,' she cried, 'I think of nothing else from morning till night!' This is the kind of obsessive thinking that can lead to depression and ill-health if nothing is done to change the pattern. Negative thinking can become a habit if we don't take positive measures to avoid it. Shirley, at last, has taken those measures. She has studied and practised mind control, which was my own salvation when I found myself on an obsessive roundabout of anxiety. I learnt that there are positive ways to control our minds, eliminating destructive thoughts and leaving us free to get the very best out of our lives. 'Most people are about as happy as they make up their minds to be', said Abraham Lincoln. Perhaps he understood the secrets of thought control; without that knowledge it can seem well-nigh impossible to escape that downward spiral of misery most of us know so well. In chapter 9, 'Getting Along with Ourselves', I shall explain these principles. We don't *have* to be a slave to our anxieties. It's up to each one of us to learn the simple techniques of self-mastery which are so essential for good relationships and a happy life.

Elderly relatives

In doing research for this book I have talked to a great many people about their difficult relationships and by far the most common problem was that of elderly relatives, especially when they were living under the same roof. I know a woman who manages a large and successful business yet her mother still treats her like a child. A friend's father is so deaf that he has the television on all day at full blast; he has his own room but nevertheless the noise echoes throughout the house. A man of forty who shares a flat with his mother because she is too nervous to live alone, cannot invite his woman friend home for a meal without causing a stormy scene. And so on. The tales of woe are endless, and I expect you could provide some further examples. When the relative lives some distance away, we may feel guilty for not visiting more often. A woman I know develops a severe migraine whenever she goes to see her cantankerous old aunt. The problem is practically insoluble. I suppose we must do what we feel is reasonable without doing so much that the quality of our own lives is at risk. If the ageing relative is very ill and totally dependent upon us, then of course the situation is quite different, especially if there are financial problems. This is a matter which hardly comes under the heading of Getting Along with People.

Other people's elderly relatives, of course, are never such a problem as our own. Family ties, although they often furnish us with warmth and love, can also generate a great deal of acrimony. When people grow old, with failing health, poor eyesight and hearing, unable to get about as they used to, they may quite understandably lose their sense of humour. Perhaps their children and grandchildren live some distance away, many of their contemporaries have died and they have had to give up the home they loved, losing their independence. Little wonder that they are hard to get along with, becoming peevish, envious and sometimes downright unpleasant. However, it seems to me that kindly and cheerful people usually age gracefully, remaining kind and cheerful to the last, but a selfish, bitter person may become more so in old age.

Having stated the problem, what advice can I offer? One thing is certain: it will demand all the compassion and patience you can muster. Not to mention humour.

If you are upbraided for neglecting elderly relatives, don't make excuses. And don't take offence if they sing high praises at great length about some friend or neighbour who visits more frequently than you do. If your appearance is criticized, say you're sorry if she doesn't like what you're wearing and that you'll try to remember to put on something else next time. This is not hypocritical, it is merely diplomatic. In delicate situations such as these, honesty is not always the best policy. Old people can be very touchy and if you want to get along with them you may have to tread rather carefully.

Be your natural self as far as possible, of course. Be warm, friendly and cheerful (but not *too* cheerful!); ask if there's any shopping you can do; remember the things they enjoy, such as looking at old photographs and talking about happy events from the past. Arrange short outings geared to their likes and capabilities. Reading aloud is often appreciated, and if the chosen book or magazine is not to your taste, don't let on!

When the conversation seems to be heading in a dangerous direction (and you will recognize the signs at once) divert it casually along more positive lines, and if you are of a volatile disposition, make a valiant effort to stay calm and relaxed under all circumstances. The provocations may be quite extreme, but when all is said and done, it's really up to you how you respond. And always remember that one day you may be in a similar position yourself (if you aren't already), hoping to get along with a younger relative and finding it far from easy.

The smoking problem

I used to smoke myself, so I can see both sides of this dilemma. I realize now that I must have given offence to non-smokers and I very much regret it. I think that, out of courtesy, smokers should refrain from lighting up without the permission of other people present. It isn't only a question of comfort but also of health; those who suffer from asthma or bronchitis, for instance, should never be compelled to breathe nicotine fumes. We all know that the danger of lung cancer is not confined to heavy smokers, but also shared by those around them. Children are particularly vulnerable. Yet if I voice these views in the mildest of terms I sometimes receive a very unfriendly response.

My advice, if you are addicted to smoking, is to go outside or into a hallway if anyone finds the smoke unpleasant. Non-smokers should not hesitate to make their feelings known, but always in a kindly way. We must never forget that many people are so seriously addicted that it seems impossible to break the habit. Others find in cigarettes a temporary relief from nervous tension; denied this relief, their distress might possibly exceed the discomfort of the non-smoker compelled to inhale their fumes. As with most problems, both large and small, the solution lies in a little more understanding on both sides, and a willingness to compromise when the situation demands it.

Finally, I would suggest hypnosis as a cure for smoking. This has often succeeded when all else failed. I am a great believer in hypnotherapy and meditation, not only as a means of relaxation but as a solution to countless health and personality problems. More of that later.

The love–hate relationship

'She's my best friend – and I hate her!' is a joke based on sound psychological truth. So is the famous old song, 'You always hurt the one you love.' It seems that love and hate are opposite sides of the same coin when it comes to human relationships. It certainly applies to lovers, whether married or not, and to parents and their offspring. Emotional closeness is bound to cause tension just *because* we care so much. The fear of losing the devotion of the beloved, the fear of being found out in some deception, the fear of not fulfilling the standards expected – in looks, accomplishments, character or behaviour – any one of these anxieties will naturally threaten our peace of mind. The solution, perhaps, is to concentrate our efforts on building up our own self-esteem so that feelings of guilt and inferiority are gradually replaced by confidence.

Nervous tension can undermine the happiness of any relationship. It's infectious. Those who suffer from it are unhappy within themselves and cause needless misery for those around them. The cure often lies in a determined assault on our own self-absorption. Outgoing people who are genuinely concerned for the comfort and happiness of others usually feel much calmer and more relaxed than those who are wrapped up in themselves, worried about their health, their looks, and what people are saying and thinking about them. We should avoid persistent requests for reassurance: 'Do you love me?' 'Do you like me better than So-and-So?' 'Will you always love me?' 'You won't be late, will you. . . ?' This kind of behaviour, signalling insecurity and dependence, may torment the beloved to such an extent that he or she can stand it no longer and leaves in search of someone who is less demanding and more self-contained. Possessiveness can ruin any loving relationhip. So can jealousy, of course, and once again the cause is usually lack of self-esteem. Those who feel unworthy of love are naturally afraid of losing it to someone better qualified to receive it! We all know that the people who are able to 'let go' of the ones they love, leaving them free to live the lives they choose, meet friends, go places on their own, and enjoy the privacy they need to develop creatively are the ones who deserve the devotion of their partners and usually retain it. Communication between lovers is always vital, and particularly so when the sexual rapport is not as it should be. We have to discuss our needs very frankly and without embarrassment if we are to get along in bed with pleasure and without distress. Sexual problems sometimes need therapy, so do look for help if your partner cannot – or will not – discuss the matter.

The best relationships blossom in an atmosphere of give-and-take in which each partner respects the other's need for independence and individuality. This applies to parents and their offspring, to those with elderly parents, to friends who live together and most of all to lovers, whether in or out of marriage. No one is entirely free from the love–hate syndrome – it seems to be an integral part of life – but we can work to keep the loving side of the coin on top as much as possible.

Giving and taking criticism

When we are learning some new skill – playing a musical instrument, speaking a foreign language, driving a car, playing chess – we take it as a matter of course that the teacher will correct our mistakes and expect us to improve as a result of criticism. We accept constructive advice, not only without rancour but with gratitude.

Not so if our *behaviour* is criticized! Yet why, if we are in search of excellence, should we welcome a friend who will help us to improve our French accent or the tone of our guitar playing, yet resent that same friend if she complains that we are thoughtless or touchy? In any good, honest relationship a certain amount of criticism can hardly be avoided; it's surely the way in which it is given and taken that makes all the difference between the useful and necessary exchange of views and a bitter argument.

Consider this example.

SHE (to her husband): You *still* haven't mended the lawnmower but you've plenty of time to watch your snooker on television.

HE: I'll mend the mower when it suits me – and if I want to watch snooker I'll damn well watch it without permission from you!

Antagonism has probably been building up for years; it may have been started by her nagging or his obstinacy, but whoever began it, it's surely up to the wiser one to create a better atmosphere.

SHE: Could you mend the lawnmower, please, love, when you've a moment? The grass is getting so long it'll be a job to cut.

Here there is no mention of snooker. This would undermine his enjoyment of watching it and make him feel guilty. Not only that, but she would feel guilty herself for having been unpleasant. The second approach is more likely to succeed and will leave them on good terms.

Here is another example.

HE (to girlfriend): I wish you wouldn't wear those ghastly ear-rings – they make you look so common.

SHE: I'll wear what I like – I think they're great.

A better way would surely be as follows.

HE: I don't think those ear-rings are quite right for you. Let's go and choose some together, shall we?

SHE: Okay – I'll wear these when you aren't around.

On the other hand, it might be better not to mention the ear-rings at all. She's a grown woman and should be free to wear what pleases her. These, of course, are examples of petty disagreements, but if people are on good terms where the trivial problems of daily life are concerned, they are more likely to comfort and support one another when serious matters arise.

People with low self-esteem are apt to be touchy if they are corrected. When a mistake is pointed out to them, even in a pleasant way, they are inclined to take it as an indictment of their whole personality. If Mrs Jones asks her timid teenage daughter to wipe her feet before coming in from the garden, the poor girl will probably sulk all day. Any form of criticism makes her feel even more unworthy. And why is she so timid? That's another story. You may like to read my book *Overcoming Shyness: A Woman's Guide*, also published by Sheldon Press. Men often undermine the confidence of their daughters, wives or girlfriends. I've seen a woman visibly tremble when her husband told her she had pronounced a word wrongly. Getting along with people means giving confidence, not taking it away, and many difficult relationships are caused by those who are so insecure that they need to put others down in order to make themselves feel powerful.

I think the answer lies in tolerance. Aren't we all inclined to expect too much of people? And sometimes of ourselves as well?

In his television *Face to Face* interview with John Freeman, Bertrand Russell said this:

Love is wise, hatred in foolish. In this world which is getting more and more closely interconnected, we have to learn to tolerate each other, we have to learn to put up with the fact that some people say things we don't like. We can only live together in that way, and if we are to live together and not die together, we must learn the kind of charity and the kind of tolerance which is absolutely vital to the continuation of human life on this planet.

8

The Workaday World

Shopping

Most of us have to cope with the workaday world, whether or not we go out to a nine-to-five job. Even a trip to the supermarket brings us up against people who could easily upset our equilibrium. There are those who jump the queue, bash us with their trolleys, knock things off shelves and don't pick them up, screech at their children or block the gangways with no thought for those who want to get past. The secret of stress-free shopping, as with all other aspects of getting along with people, must surely lie within ourselves – our personal attitude to the inevitable irritations and our thoughtfulness for others.

However considerate you may be yourself, you are constantly faced by tired or neurotic folk who cannot or will not play their part in making life as easy and pleasant as possible. Some people simply do not *care* how much trouble they cause. They have probably been subjected to such unkindness – or even cruelty – that they get a perverse pleasure out of being difficult. They subconsciously believe that they deserve to suffer and they invite friction when there's no need for it. 'I'm not happy,' they seem to think, 'so why should anyone else be?'

I have said in chapter 7 that I think we should avoid nervous tension as far as possible by disregarding most of the offensive behaviour we encounter in the workaday world. If a woman bangs your leg with her supermarket trolley you can shout at her or give her a hard angry stare; or you can take no notice, try to ignore the pain, and remind yourself that there must have been occasions when you have accidentally hurt someone with a trolley. If you take the last option you will go on your way feeling more relaxed than if you flared up angrily.

'No way!' you may be thinking. 'I'd feel a lot better if I gave her a piece of my mind!' That's a matter of opinion. Resentment can do us a lot of damage and if we make a determined effort not to get rattled we shall reduce the wear and tear on our nerves and feel a great deal better in every way. We can't avoid a certain amount of stress but our health may suffer unless we learn to keep relaxed and calm when things go wrong.

Let me tell you about The Gas Lady. Some years ago we had continual trouble with our cooker, and I had to make a great many visits to the local gas showroom to explain that yet another man had brought the wrong part, didn't know how to fit it, or that no-one had come at all. The woman in the showroom had a very unpleasant manner. She never smiled. Sometimes she took no notice of me at all for several minutes, treating me as if I had no right to be there. Her tone of voice was cold and scathing although I tried my best to be brief and polite. I dreaded going, but as our cooker was out of action there was nothing else for it.

Then one day I arrived there a few minutes before closing time and for some reason, while she was writing down my latest complaint, I said to her: 'You must be tired, being on your feet all day.' She didn't respond, but the next time I went in, her attitude was completely different. She almost smiled and even apologized for the terrible service I was receiving. All she had needed, of course, was for someone to care, *to be on her side*. Isn't that what we all want – for people to be on our side? She may have had appalling personal problems to cope with at home, and I wished I'd made a point of speaking kindly to her weeks before.

The relationship between shop assistants and customers is a delicate one whichever side of the counter you're on. Both parties are probably tired, and we all know that when we are overwrought we are not ourselves. The assistants have been coping for hours with customers who must be 'always right', however difficult; the shopper has probably been trailing from store to store, searching for the required articles at a sensible price, perhaps with a fractious child in tow. Getting along with people in shops is full of hazards and we all need to make a special effort to be patient and good humoured.

At work

Offices, factories, shops, schools, hospitals, hotels and many other workplaces demand enormous resilience and diplomacy if we are to be happy there. Most people spend so much of their lives at work that it's vitally important to develop good relationships with those around them.

Humour always helps. If you can laugh *at* yourself and *with* your colleagues you'll be more than half-way there. Be prepared to accept a certain amount of teasing and don't be upset by vulgarity or bad language; they're bound to crop up. Touchy people always get more than a fair share of jibes because they are seen to be vulnerable. It's a hard world, this workaday world, and we have to be quite tough to withstand the pressures. Most of us are keen to make a good impression, not only because we need to keep our jobs and earn promotion but because we want to be popular. Everyone needs affection and respect, however much they may pretend they don't care.

The best practical advice I can offer is to work hard to keep on top of the job. If you feel confident in this respect you'll be less anxious and have more energy left to devote to the vital task of relating to others. If anyone is in difficulties, do all you can to help. Listen patiently to their problems. Give them a little of your valuable time. And don't hesitate to ask for advice yourself; we should never be afraid to admit to our ignorance. If we fail to perform our tasks efficiently, who knows what inconvenience – or even danger – our failure might cause? Everybody makes mistakes from time to time and we shouldn't feel dispirited when we are corrected, but if we are constantly in difficulties it's time to ask ourselves if we are in the right job. It takes courage to change, especially when unemployment is rife, but it's miserably self-destructive to spend our precious days on something that gives us no satisfaction. 'But I need the money!' you may protest. I know it's a terrible dilemma, but happiness is more important than money and this is a vital truth we need to keep in mind – when there's a choice.

If you hate your work and long for each day to be over, ask yourself *why*. Here are some possible reasons, with suggestions for solving the problem.

1. You don't feel competent to do the job

This could be because you haven't had sufficient training or do not properly understand what is required of you. You may need further study, expert advice or simply more experience. Do something positive to build up the confidence and efficiency you need.

2. You are not the right person for the job

You may be temperamentally or physically unsuited for the work you have taken on. Do you find it uninteresting? Most tasks are boring from time to time, but perhaps yours is totally tedious. On the other hand, it may be too demanding. Is it a dead-end job with no possibility of advancement? Does it entail too much travelling? Are the hours too long? Is there some other work that attracts you a great deal more? If any of these problems apply to you, I'd recommend a change. Soon.

3. You don't get on very well with your colleagues

Is there something in your manner that causes antagonism? Are you inclined to be bossy, to lose your temper, to make people feel guilty? Do you gossip too much? Do you sulk? Or moan? Or flirt? Do you run people down? Are you negative in your outlook? An honest answer to these questions could pinpoint your weaknesses and help you to create a friendlier atmosphere.

4. You don't like your boss

This isn't an easy one. Bosses can't be removed by their

subordinates and one usually has to stick it out. Be as pleasant as possible and try to relax at the first sign of tension. Keep on top of your work, don't give in to resentment, and make your feelings known to her firmly but politely. It could be that she hadn't realized there was a problem, and will gladly try to do something about it. If things are really bad, you can comfort yourself with the knowledge that bosses do get promotion (or demotion) and move on to other departments and other branches.

5. *You are in a position of authority and you feel you are unpopular with your subordinates*

Analyse the possible reasons. Do you expect too much of them, overwork them or give too little praise? Perhaps you're over-critical, not sufficiently tolerant when mistakes are made? Do you refuse to delegate, not trusting anyone else to be accurate? How's your sense of humour? There's nothing like a good laugh from time to time to lighten the working day, and if the boss has a sense of fun it will infect everyone's mood. As with number 3, check on your manner, trying to picture yourself as others see you.

6. *You lack self-confidence*

If you feel shy and inadequate, without quite knowing why, I suggest you read my book *Overcoming Shyness: A Woman's Guide*, in which I analyse in detail the causes of shyness and explain how it can be mastered. Self-assurance is vital if you are to enjoy your work, whatever it may be.

We all need a great deal of sympathetic understanding, and the more help and encouragement we can give to those who work alongside us, the higher our self-esteem will be and the more we shall feel at home in the workaday world.

Commuting

Queues, crowds, luggage and delays are inevitable, but a good rapport with our fellow-sufferers can make it all a great deal more bearable. If you smile sympathetically, for instance, at a woman on the train with a crying baby, it will help her to feel less guilty about the noise it's making. If you move up readily when somebody wants to sit down, shift your bag out of the way, shut sliding doors after you, help elderly people with their cases if you are young and healthy (and even offer them your seat) – this kind of courtesy and kindness will make life easier for everyone.

If you drive to work, fatigue is the main problem. When you are tired in the evening, longing to get home and caught in a rush-hour tailback, it isn't easy to stay relaxed. No seasoned motorist wants to be told how to drive, and I hesitate to give advice, but I have been a member of the Institute of Advanced Motorists for nearly thirty years, so I hope you'll forgive me for offering a few reminders.

Ill-temper at the wheel can cause an accident. We all know it's true, yet many excellent drivers allow their anger to get in the way of their efficiency. If you are fuming about someone ahead who is doing a steady 25 m.p.h. in the middle of the road, a dare-devil overtaking dangerously or a pedestrian who steps off the pavement without looking, you could fail to notice a child who runs out suddenly to chase a ball. Resentment is the enemy of good driving, and it seems to me that conscious relaxation is the best solution (see chapter 9). If our blood pressure goes up every time another motorist annoys us, we are bound to lose concentration. And if we blow our tops about it to our passengers we shall spoil their journey as well as putting their lives at risk!

I think we should never sound our horns unless we need to do so for safety. Nobody likes the driver who hoots impatiently in a traffic jam. And motorists often give cause for annoyance by driving too close to the vehicle in front; a glance at those stopping distances in the Highway Code, probably long forgotten, will remind us of the dangers.

Don't forget to switch to dipped headlights in bad weather (sidelights alone are insufficient) and light up in good time at dusk. If you are present at an accident, even if it's nothing serious, do get out and offer yourself as a witness. It's so easy to drive on, forgetting that your words of support could make all the difference to the innocent person's insurance claim if no-one else is prepared to testify. One day you may be grateful to someone who will give up their time to help you in this way.

We all make mistakes at the wheel from time to time – going down a one-way street, driving badly when we're lost, making a mess of our parking, scraping a gatepost – but lack of concentration is usually the cause, and this is something we can all improve on. Small children and dogs in the car can be a serious distraction unless they are trained to be good passengers. Last week I saw a big dog in the car in front licking the back of the driver's neck!

I hardly need to mention the appalling hazard of the drinking driver. We all know the problem, and if you enjoy a drink, as I do, you must listen to the voice of your own wise conscience whenever you are tempted. One more glass of wine could be a matter of life or death. How would we live with ourselves if we killed a child – or caused any kind of injury – just because we couldn't resist another drink?

I'd like to end this chapter with another quotation from *Psycho-Cybernetics* by Dr Maxwell Maltz.

Your physical body has a built-in thermostat which maintains your inner physical temperature at a steady 98.6 degrees, regardless of the temperature of the environment. The weather around you may be freezing cold, or 110 degrees, yet your body maintains its own climate. . . . You also have a built-in spiritual thermostat which enables you to maintain an emotional climate and atmosphere in spite of the emotional weather around you. Many people do not use this spiritual thermostat because they do not know it is there; they do not know such a thing is possible, and they do not understand that they do *not* have to take on the outward climate. Yet, your spiritual thermostat is just as necessary for emotional health and well-being as your physical thermostat is for physical health.

It may seem well-nigh impossible to use this kind of mental equipment when we have to deal with difficult people and stressful situations, but I promise it is only a matter of confidence and perseverance. In the next chapter we shall see how it can be done.

9

Getting Along with Ourselves

Getting along with other people could be described as resolving conflicts, creating harmony and having a reasonably happy time together. As I see it, getting along with ourselves calls for the same kind of relationship between the different aspects of our own personality. If we are dissatisfied with the proportion of dark and light, negative and positive, selfish and caring, then we cannot get along very well with ourselves. It follows that we also find it difficult to relate to others.

The psychologists tell us that we can't like other people unless we like ourselves, and I'm sure that's true. Liking oneself, in the best sense, does not imply vanity or self-adulation. It just means rejoicing in our own true identity, trying to live up to our ideals and even though we often fail to do so, recognizing our weaknesses and making a serious effort to overcome them. Guilt is one of the greatest enemies, reducing our self-esteem and making us unsure of ourselves in relation to those we meet. It is often imposed quite needlessly at an early age by a domineering or over-critical parent or teacher. If this is your problem, remind yourself that you are no longer a child at the mercy of a restrictive adult; you are a person in your own right and there is really no need to carry the burden of guilt for another minute.

Sometimes an over-demanding partner might have created a sense of worthlessness – and indeed may still be doing so. If you sincerely desire to gain the self-assurance and freedom of spirit that is your birthright, you will have to make a courageous effort to change the pattern. You may not be able to break away to freedom – perhaps you don't even want to – but at least you can develop fresh interests, make new friends and gradually emerge from the sense of isolation you may feel. Many women are under the domination of a difficult man, and unless they take positive action to assert their rights, they will grow more and more submissive, more frustrated and, inevitably, more resentful. It might not be easy to branch out in new directions – family and lack of funds can seem insuperable problems – but the future begins today and wasted weeks are never returned to us.

If you are feeling guilty on account of something you have done or left undone, face up to it and do all you can to make amends including, of course, a sincere apology. If this is impossible, try to put the matter out of your mind; with thought control it is not so difficult as it may appear to be. Living in the present is the secret; regrets and anxieties serve no useful purpose, they only wreck your peace of mind and undermine your health. But if we resolve not to repeat our mistakes and to plan a more positive approach to the future, our confidence will grow. Those who feel guilty are inclined to be defensive and this makes them hard to get along with; they often take offence when none is meant.

People with low self-esteem are often anxious in case people won't like them, and so they avoid the very situations that would provide the opportunities for rewarding new friendships. They don't really know what ails them; they seem to drive people away and yet they don't know why. They are often lonely and miserable when there is no need to be. In most cases (though some will obviously require professional therapy) a little honest self-assessment could change their lives. 'The only way to have a friend,' said Emerson, 'is to be one.'

Awareness and response

We are very much aware of our own feelings – misunderstood, insulted, ignored – but sometimes we are not sufficiently aware of other people's. Our responses, so vital in human relationships, will always depend on our understanding of others. Resentment is poison, sympathy is balm, yet if our resentment is justified we may feel that it is inescapable. The answer lies in the power, possessed by all of us but seldom used, to control our thoughts through meditation and auto-suggestion. Relaxation is the first essential, the kind of deep relaxation that produces calm and confidence. This is an ability we can acquire with practice – perhaps from a hypnotherapist, a tape recording or Yoga classes – enabling us to substitute peace of mind for resentment and nervous tension. Needless to say, it takes time and perseverance if these ideas are new to you, but the rewards are truly amazing: better health, deeper contentment and the gradual phasing out of bad feeling, at least on *our* side. It isn't easy to change other people (perhaps we shouldn't try) but we can certainly change our own responses to the pressures they impose upon us. When we are free from tension we seem to bring out the best in people. It's as if they sense that we present no threat and that we want to understand and be helpful. If we are under stress we alert the tension in others, and good communication may become impossible.

Mind control is essential; without it we can hardly hope to withstand the hurts which are, for most of us, an inescapable part of life. Meditation, faithfully practised, provides a built-in defence against all manner of barbs and distressing suggestions. 'You'll never pass that exam,' someone may tell us. Or: 'You'll be worn out if you do that'. Or: 'You'll never manage that journey on your own.' Perhaps you are giving *yourself* negative suggestions? 'I'm sure to get one of my headaches when So-and-So comes.' Or: 'I'll never finish such-and-such in time'. Or: 'I shan't sleep a wink until I get that letter . . .'. The vast majority of people bombard themselves with negative suggestions quite unconsciously, totally unaware of the self-injury they are inflicting.

I used to be the same – and suffered in consequence – until I went to a hypnotherapist in 1972. He taught me how to practice self-hypnosis, replacing negative ideas with positive ones, and the benefits were fantastic. Headaches became a thing of the past; I needed no more tranquillizers or sleeping pills; I grew healthier and happier in every way. And so long as I remember to do my self-hypnosis for fifteen minutes twice a day, I am free from the tensions and ailments that had plagued me for so many years. The power to control our own equilibrium, as Dr Maltz has said, is within ourselves, and needless to say it is invaluable when it comes to personal relationships. You are not a slave to your own negative self-suggestions; your thoughts are for *you* to decide and you can begin to establish a positive pattern this very day.

In his marvellous book *The Silva Mind Control Method*, José Silva has this to say:

> Something beautiful happens in meditation, and the beauty you find is calming. The more you meditate, the deeper you go within yourself, the firmer the grasp you will have of a kind of inner peace so strong that nothing in life will be able to shatter it.
>
> Your body will benefit, too. At first you will find that worries and guilt feelings are absent while you are meditating. One of the beauties of meditation at the Alpha level is that you *cannot* bring your feelings of guilt and anger with you. If these feelings intrude you will simply pop out of the meditative level. As time goes on, they will stay away longer, until one day they are gone for good. This means that those activities of the mind that make our bodies sick will be neutralised. The body is designed to be healthy. It has its own healing mechanisms built in. These mechanisms are blocked by minds not trained to control themselves. Meditation is the first step in Mind Control; by itself it will go a long way toward setting free the body's healing powers and giving it back the energy once squandered on tension.

This book is high on my list of recommended reading for anyone who feels unsure of themselves. The idea of practising meditation regularly may seem quite alien – and even unacceptable – to some of my readers, but it is not in conflict with any religion and is a widely recognized treatment for all ailments related to stress and anxiety. When you reach that state of deep tranquillity known as the Alpha level, your subconscious mind, which can be a veritable maelstrom of nervous fears, is receptive to your positive suggestions. The feeling of security and peace can only be properly understood by those who have experienced it. No possible harm can result; only the gradual elimination of needless regrets and anxious speculations.

You might like to read the excellent book *Teach Yourself Meditation* by James Hewitt who is also a Yoga teacher. There are many ways in which you can reach the Alpha level. A simple introduction is to sit or lie in a comfortable position, close your eyes and count slowly backwards from a hundred to one. As you concentrate on counting, you will find that extraneous thoughts gradually disperse, to be replaced by a sensation of deep calm, quite different from the kind of relaxation you experience when you merely flop down in a chair and try to let go of your tensions. You may prefer to count your breaths from one to ten, returning to number one every time you lose concentration. Don't be discouraged if you can't get to ten straight away; it took me several weeks before I succeeded in banishing intrusive thoughts. But when I did, the skill was established and now I find that I can reach the Alpha level at once and give myself the helpful suggestions I need. And of course it's a marvellous method for getting to sleep if you suffer from insomnia.

Creative visualization

This is a well-known method of healing and has remarkably curative results, even in the treatment of cancer. The power of the imagination, when we are deeply relaxed at the Alpha level of mind, is known to have an astounding effect on our physical well-being and on our general behaviour. Many sportsmen and sportswomen use it and have proved beyond doubt the importance of mental attitudes in their profession. We've all seen snooker, golf or tennis champions lose confidence and fluff the easiest of shots.

Tell yourself that you'll sleep like a top tonight and the chances are that you will. But tell yourself that you're sure to lie awake for hours worrying about such-and-such and you'll bring about the very thing you fear. Your imagination dictates the behaviour of your body to an incredible degree. When you are facing a situation that has proved difficult in the past, picture yourself, very clearly, in your mind's eye, as you want to be – relaxed and confident – and you will hardly believe how faithfully that positive image of yourself is realized when the time arrives. I do a considerable amount of lecturing and when I expect a large audience, which might be a little daunting, I meditate beforehand and picture myself on the platform, looking and feeling happy and relaxed, able to find the words I need, coping easily with any difficult questions. If I have to face a meeting with someone who is likely to upset me, a long drive, a visit to the dentist, or any hazard large or small, I picture myself as I would like to be. Nine times out of ten, it works. The tenth time is probably the one when I didn't concentrate sufficiently or didn't really believe it would work. You must have confidence. Did you realize that the word confidence really means 'with faith' (Latin *con fides*)? Another reason for failure is bringing the *will* into play, rather than the *imagination*. In his book *Self Mastery through Conscious Autosuggestion*, Emile Coué writes:

> It is the imagination and not the will which is the most important faculty of man; and thus it is a serious mistake to advise people to train their wills, it is the training of their imaginations which they ought to set about. . . . By believing oneself to be the master of one's thoughts one becomes so.

So it is that when we very much want a meeting to run smoothly but feel sure that it won't (that is, *imagine* it won't), we are setting the scene for failure. If on the contrary we picture things going well, tell ourselves with confidence that we shall feel great and they *will* go well, then we are geared for success. In all probability, depending on our understanding and experience of meditation or self-hypnosis, the results will be exactly as we want them to be – or even better than we dared to dream. There are wonderful powers at work in our lives, as many of you will know very well. Sometimes our apprehensions seem to get in the way, blocking that pipeline to the Source. The body reacts to needless fear just as surely as it reacts to justified fear; if you *think* there's a burglar in the house when it's only a shutter rattling in the wind, you're just as frightened as if there really were one.

It can take a little time – weeks or even months – to train oneself along the lines suggested by Emile Coué, José Silva and a great many other sages of the past and present, but a sustained programme of meditation can bring about a near miracle in your life, as it did in mine. You can cure yourself of all manner of physical ailments and establish a sense of peace and security, even though the circumstances seem to make happiness impossible.

Harmonious relationships are vital to our well-being, and the efforts we make to improve the difficult ones can enrich our lives in all kinds of unexpected ways. Surely there is nothing more rewarding than the giving and taking of kindness and understanding. You *can* get along with people. It's up to you . . .

Further Reading

Berne, Eric, *Games People Play*. Penguin 1970.

Birnbaum, Jack, *How to Stop Hating and Start Loving*. Pan 1975.

Coleman, Vernon, *How to Stop Feeling Guilty*. Sheldon Press 1982.

Coué, Emile, *Self Mastery Through Conscious Auto-suggestion*. Unwin Hyman 1922.

Cox, Gill & Dainow, Sheila, *Making the Most of Loving*. Sheldon Press 1988.

Cox, Gill & Dainow, Sheila, *Making the Most of Yourself*. Sheldon Press 1985.

Doubtfire, Dianne, *Overcoming Shyness: A Woman's Guide*. Sheldon Press 1988.

Gibran, Kahlil, *The Prophet*. Pan 1980.

Harris, Tom, *I'm OK – You're OK*. Pan 1973.

Hauck, Paul, *Calm Down*. Sheldon Press 1980.

Hauck, Paul, *How to Love and Be Loved*. Sheldon Press 1983.

Hauck, Paul, *How to Be Your Own Best Friend*. Sheldon Press 1988.

Hewitt, James, *Teach Yourself Meditation*. Hodder & Stoughton 1978.

Hewitt, James, *Yoga and You*. Tandem 1966.

Honey, Peter, *Solving Your Personal Problems*. Sheldon Press 1983.

Maltz, Maxwell, *Psycho-Cybernetics*. Prentice-Hall, U.S.A. 1967.

Manning, Matthew, *Matthew Manning's Guide to Self-Healing*. Thorsons 1989.

Markham, Ursula, *Hypnothink*. Thorsons 1985.

Nelson, Margaret, *Someone to Love*. Sheldon Press 1988.

Peale, Norman Vincent, *A Guide to Confident Living*.

World's Work Ltd, U.S.A. 1955.

Peale, Norman Vincent, *The Power of Positive Thinking*. World's Work Ltd, U.S.A. 1963.

Pease, Allan, *Body Language*. Sheldon Press 1984.

Roet, Brian, *All in the Mind?* Optima 1987.

Silva, José, *The Silva Mind Control Method*. Souvenir Press 1980.

Waxman, David, *Hypnosis*. Unwin Paperbacks 1981.

Relaxation Tapes are available from:

Institute of Tape Learning
P.O. Box 4
Hemel Hempstead
Herts

The Matthew Manning Centre
39 Abbeygate Street
Bury St Edmunds
Suffolk IP33 1LW

People Products Ltd
141 Albany Road
Earlsdon
Coventry CV5 6ND